I0825184

The PERSISTENCE

The PERSISTENCE

How Scott Presler Cleaned Up America's Cities, Seized the Voter Registration Movement from Democrats, and Helped to Elect Donald Trump

Scott Presler

War Room Books may be purchased in bulk at special discounts for sales promotion, corporate gifts, fund-raising, or educational purposes. Special editions can also be created to specifications. For details, contact the Special Sales Department, Skyhorse Publishing, 307 Fifth Avenue, 4th Floor, New York, NY 10016 or info@skyhorsepublishing.com.

War Room Books® and Skyhorse® and Skyhorse Publishing® are registered trademarks of Skyhorse Publishing, Inc.®, a Delaware corporation.

Visit our website at www.skyhorsepublishing.com.

10 9 8 7 6 5 4 3 2 1

Library of Congress Cataloging-in-Publication Data is available on file.

Cover design by David Ter-Avanesyan
Cover photo credit: Scott Presler

Print ISBN: 978-1-64821-229-1
Ebook ISBN: 978-1-64821-231-4

Printed in the United States of America

CONTENTS

INTRODUCTION

In 2024, Donald J. Trump held his second to last campaign rally in Pittsburgh, Pennsylvania. Pennsylvania was the battleground state. It had nineteen Electoral College votes. For the past decade, Democrats and Republicans had been at war with each other to seize those votes. In 2016, Trump defeated Hillary Clinton by forty-thousand votes. In 2020, Joe Biden defeated Trump by eighty thousand votes. I moved to Pennsylvania in 2024 to re-elect Trump to the White House. I knew it was going to be a war, but it was a war we could win.

On the night before the election, I was driving home at around eleven o'clock. I had just been at President Trump's rally in Pittsburgh. My phone rang. It was Lara Trump. In the lead-up to the 2024 election, Lara and I had become close allies. She shared my vision to Make America Great Again, and she also understood that this was an election we absolutely had to win. Like me, she wasn't in politics to tweet, or to post on Facebook, or to take a photograph for Instagram. She was in it to save our country. So, when I saw her name pop up on my phone, I knew it was important.

"Hey, Lara! What can I do for you?"

"Scott!" she exclaimed, "I have someone here who wants to talk to you."

Even amidst the background noise on her end—it sounded like a jet was about to take off into the sky—the voice on the other end of the line was unmistakable.

"Hey Scott! It's your biggest fan! It's President Trump!

"Mr. President!" I answered, "We're working tirelessly for you in Pennsylvania!"

"That's great, Scott! How's it looking? How do you think we'll do in Pennsylvania?"

Pennsylvania. Pennsylvania. Pennsylvania.

On the eve of the election, it was the state on everyone's mind. I knew how important this state was. Lara Trump knew how important this state was. President Trump, about to take off on his jet to the final rally in Michigan, knew how absolutely important this state was to the 2024 election.

"Mr. President," I said, "your early voting is good. It looks like we're hitting the numbers that we need to hit in Philadelphia. We need to get 20 percent of Philadelphia to win. It looks like we're going to do it. We also need to do well in Pittsburgh. We need to get 40 percent of Pittsburgh to take Allegheny County. I think we're going to do it, Mr. President. I think we're going to win this election!"

The liberal media paints President Trump as an egotist, a narcissist, and someone who would rather hear himself speak than listen to anyone else. But my own experience with the president couldn't be further from that fiction. He's a man who is deeply interested in the perspectives of those around him. He's a man who wants to learn. As my car barreled down I-279, the president of the United States just listened.

"We need those rural voters, Mr. President. We need to get them out to the polls. You will win if we get our rurals out because they offset the big cities. If our farmers, and our beautiful Amish, and all the people who make Pennsylvania great come out to the polls, we won't need to win Philadelphia or Pittsburgh."

As that jet revved its engines and our phone call came to a close, I could not have been more confident. That night, I posted to X: "Mr. President we're going to deliver Pennsylvania for you."

I was right.

On March 3, 2025, I was invited to the Oval Office to meet President Trump and Vice President JD Vance. In a now viral photo, the two of us flank the president on each side as he sits behind the Hayes desk. I wasn't invited to the Oval Office because I'm a famous pundit like Sean Hannity. I wasn't invited because I'm a famous athlete like Tom Brady, or a famous musician like Kid Rock, or a famous comedian like Theo Von.

I was invited because—in the world of politics—I get things done.

This is a book about how I got things done in Pennsylvania, in Baltimore, and in cities and states across America. It's a book about how my team and I seized the voter registration movement from the Democratic Party. It's a book about how Donald Trump's victories in 2016, 2020, and 2024 changed the direction of this country.

It's a book about what the Republican Party needs to do to win in 2026, 2028, and beyond.

Chapter 1

THE MAKING OF A GRASSROOTS ACTIVIST

The Pulse Night Club Massacre

I'll be gosh darn honest: I don't look or act like your typical Republican. I'm six-foot-five inches tall. I wear leather cowboy boots that make me appear even taller. I have long, silky dark hair that hangs down my waist. I once posted a TikTok video of me straightening my hair with a flat iron while listening to "Starships" by Nicki Minaj. I don't think anyone looks at me and thinks, "He must be a conservative!"

On June 12, 2016, I was working for the Republican Party of Virgina. I wasn't publicly out of the closet, yet. But I'm sure within two seconds of talking to me, people probably guessed that I wasn't bumping Nicki Minaj because I was attracted to her! Anyway, I was down in Virginia Beach working to elect President Trump, and we got news that yet another radical Islamic terrorist had once again opened fire on a crowd of innocent Americans inside our beautiful country.

This time, we learned that the mass shooting occurred inside a gay nightclub in Orlando, Florida. That night—all over the news, all over social media—everyone was talking about it. The Democrats were telling Americans they shouldn't jump to conclusions about Islam, as if Muslims, Jews, Catholics, and the Amish are all opening fire on innocent people with the same regularity. Bless their hearts!

Conservatives, for their part, were rightly pointing out that this is what happens when America is weak on terrorism. Led by President Barack Obama and Vice President Sleepy Joe Biden, a vice president who couldn't tell you what he had for breakfast much less what we should do about the growing number of terrorist cells around the world aspiring to turn the United States into rubble, the government had once again failed to keep Americans safe.

What was worse was that the Democrats were exploiting this atrocious shooting to advance their own political interests. On TikTok, on Facebook, on Instagram, and on YouTube, I was seeing messages from liberals that were linking this terrorist attack to the upcoming election in November. Remember when Sleepy Joe said, "Well, I tell you what, if you have a problem figuring out whether you're for me or Trump, then you ain't Black"? People were saying something similar about Hillary Clinton. The resounding message was that even more gun restrictions, brought to you by the Democratic Party, were what was going to keep gay Americans, like the victims of the Pulse night club shooting, safe. In plain English: if you had a problem figuring out if you were for Hillary Clinton or Donald J. Trump, then you weren't gay.

At this point, I was used to the Democrats pandering to "marginalized people" like me. But this latest attempt struck a particular chord with me. Frankly, it was appalling how the Democrats were using this massacre—brought to you by their restrictive gun laws and milquetoast foreign policy—to help elect one of the most corrupt people in the history of American politics. Moreover, the liberals who were purporting to be on the side of gays were ruthlessly trashing us.

Across social media, there were people who were saying that they were gay and they were going to vote for Trump. On Twitter, the hashtag #GaysForTrump was trending. The liberals—who will bark at you all day long about how loving, inclusive, and tolerant they are—were attacking these people! They were posting responses like "#GaysForTrump is like #SnailsForSalt." "It's like #ChickensForKFC." "It like #VampiresForGarlic." There wasn't anything respectful about it. There was just this pervasive liberal condescension, so thick you could cut it with a knife. If you were a gay American who wanted to see Trump elected to the Oval Office, in their eyes you were a complete and decisive idiot.

Meanwhile, here I am—a gay man reeling from a terrorist attack that I feel personally connected to in a deep way—being treated like a low-IQ moron who, apparently, doesn't understand my own interests. In that moment, I was over it. So I decided to come out of the closet on social media. At the time, my hair wasn't long. I wasn't yet rocking my leather cowboy boots. I had about twenty to thirty thousand followers. By comparison, I have more than two million followers on X now, and I'm regularly recognized in public for my trademark hair and boots.

But at the time, I was still looking great. I had a wonderful shag going, just a bit of curl in my hair on the edges. I was rocking a Make America Great Again hat, kind of tilted to the side a little bit. I had a black tank top on, my arms were showing, and I had my nice traps poking out a little. I had that skater boy look going on. (If you can't bear these fashion asides, this might not be the book for you.) I'm not going to lie, I was looking great and I was fired up when I snapped a photo of myself. "We do exist," I wrote, alongside that big, beautiful, trending hashtag: #GaysForTrump.

My post spread like wildfire! It was liberating. It was authentic. And the response from my fellow Republicans made it the best day of my life. All these Christian evangelical Trump supporters—who liberals cast as maniacal homophobes—said they had my back. It didn't matter if they were from Southern California or rural New Hampshire, the message was crystal clear: the Make America Great Again movement was glad to have Scott Presler, an openly gay American with his hat tilted to the side like a skater boy, on their team.

That was also the day the thin veil of tolerance that the Democratic Party wears was lifted right in front of my eyes. Members of that party, which purports to be carrying the beacon of love, respect, anti-bigotry, anti-misogyny, and anti-homophobia—basically everything that is good in the world—sent me death threats. I had left the plantation where all the gays were supposed to be, and the liberals were angry. According to their narrative, gay Americans should be obedient to the Hillary Clintons, Joe Bidens, and Kamala Harrises of the world. They shouldn't think for themselves. They certainly should not be casting their vote for a "homophobic fascist in a red trucker hat."

My viral post, which had thousands of reposts and likes, connected to so many people, many of whom were sick and tired of the Democrats' superficial commitment to gay Americans. By January 2017, I had fifty thousand followers. These followers—who are gay, who are not gay, who are Christians, who are atheists, who have voted Republican their whole lives, who have just left the Democratic Party—don't care that I'm gay.

Unlike the Left, who wants to divide us by race, gender, and sexuality, the Right doesn't reduce me to my gayness. It values my authenticity more than my identity. From the day I came out on social media, I have tried my best to remain authentic. Even now, with millions of followers, I'm still writing my own tweets. I'm still traveling the country. I'm still connecting with people on the streets. And I'm still calling out the Democrats' baloney when I see it.

Speaking of baloney, Hillary Clinton takes money from countries that murder gay people. That's not rhetoric. That's a fact. When she exclaimed that "gay rights are human rights and human rights are gay rights," I couldn't help but wonder if she had ever talked to a gay person who lives in Saudia Arabia. The last time I checked, homosexuality is illegal and punishable under the Wahhabist interpretation of Sharia law, which is the basis of that country's legal system. The last time I checked, the Clinton Foundation received millions of dollars from the Kingdom of Saudi Arabia. The last time I checked, the father of the Islamic terrorist who shot up the Pulse night club was seen at a Clinton rally, held just thirty minutes from the Pulse night club. This is the political candidate who gay Americans like me are supposed to rally behind? In what kind of bizarro world does that make sense?

I mean, really, just contrast Crooked Hillary's political babble with Donald Trump's comments after the shooting. One of the many things people love about our president is his directness. He's not reading notes off a teleprompter written by a graduate of Amherst College. He's blunt, he's often politically incorrect, and he tells it like it is. President Trump will not hesitate to call a spade a spade. "A radical Islamic terrorist targeted the night club. Not only because he wanted to kill Americans, but in order to execute gay and lesbian citizens because of their sexual orientation. It's a strike at the heart and soul of who we are as a nation." As he more succinctly put it in a tweet, "Thank you to the LGBT community! I will fight for you while Hillary brings in more people that will threaten your freedoms and beliefs."

When Donald Trump, then the president-elect, called for an "ideological screening test" for immigrants "who believe that Sharia law should supplant American law," it said more about the MAGA movement's commitment to gay people than all the liberal identity blather I had heard my entire life. For liberals, adding additional letters to LGBT (now we're at LGBTQIA2S+) and more colors to the pride flag (why is brown in a rainbow?) is what supporting gays looks like. For Republicans, supporting gays means protecting us from religious fanatics who, quite literally, want to murder us. Call me crazy, but I don't want my country flooded with Islamic extremists who would absolutely love to throw me off a three-story roof. Christians may not bake me a cake for my wedding, but they are not going to throw me off a building. In America, gays talk metaphorically about living in the closet. In the Middle East, they are literally living in the closet. If common sense is what counts as conservative these days, then please keep me away from liberals.

For Republicans, supporting gays also means defending our constitutional right to protect ourselves. I'm a pretty boy, but I'm also an alpha male in more ways than one. I love going to gun shows. I love going to the shooting range. I love picking up the latest issue of *Guns and Ammo*. I think there's a stereotype about gays that's been perpetuated by the liberal media. In that view, we're all feeble, rainbow-wearing beta males who twerk and flick our wrists.

In reality, many of us could protect ourselves with a single bullet—peacefully. In fact, many of us would have stopped Omar Mateen from firing one single bullet. Islamic terrorists like him are always going to have access to guns. As long as Democrats are in power, they're also going to have access to our country. By the way, did you know that Omar Mateen's father, Seddique Mateen, was an FBI informant? Did you also know that Seddique Mateen was seated behind Hillary Clinton at one of her rallies in Kissimmee, Florida, *after* the Pulse nightclub terror attack? Isn't it amazing how many FBI informants have been tied to terrorism? But I digress.

I say, "Arm the gays!"

Look, I get it. I'm a non-traditional Republican. I'm a long-haired, boot-wearing, gay man who knows all the words to more than one Lady Gaga song. But I'm also a Catholic. I'm from the south. I was born in Florida and raised in Virginia. My dad is a retired captain in the United States Navy. His father was a US Navy captain, too. I grew up around men who lived lives of courage and service. They wanted to serve this beautiful country. All of that is a part of me, in the same way my long-haired, boot-wearing identity is a part of me. I'm the bridge that helps our Christian evangelicals connect with the growing number of gay conservatives. I'm the bridge that connects those on the furthest ends of the right wing to the more moderate center of the Republican Party. I'm the guy who builds bridges between the Amish, and conservative moms, and the burly men with beards rocking camouflage fatigues and orange hats at the gun shows. Just as my grandfather and my father were leading different groups of people on the open seas, I'm leading different groups of people around the country, from all walks of life, to the voting booth. I'm here to serve America—first.

To this day, I'll have straight married men who will slide into my DMs to just say, "You know, Scott, you have opened my eyes, and I want to let you know that I support you, and I'm as proud of you as if you were my own son." My inbox is just flooded with messages of support, positivity, and love. It really is constant, and it's actually a little bit overwhelming. There's still a stereotype about Republicans. Look at me. How could I be a representative for the Christian faith? How could I understand the Second Amendment? But that stereotype is fading away fast—and with it the idea that people who look, talk, and act like me are going to continue to give their uncritical support to the Democratic Party. The Democrats want to divide people by their identities. I want to unite people. I want to build bridges between gays, and straights, and the Amish, and the frat boys, and the neoconservatives, and the America First conservatives like me. Above all, I want to continue to make America great again.

I would vote for a paper bag before I'd vote for a Democrat. I truly believe the worst Republican is better than the best Democrat. Back in 2016, the Democrats said Hillary Clinton was leading The Resistance. In fact, Hillary herself said she was still involved in The Resistance after she was unambiguously defeated by the American people in 2016. In an interview after the election, she said, "I'm now back to being an activist citizen and part of The Resistance." Her audience clapped and cheered. The *Babylon Bee*, the right-wing version of the *Onion*, once ran a headline, "Man Who Agrees with the Media, Universities, Corporations, And Hollywood Thinks He's Part Of The Resistance." If they had changed the title of that article to "woman," it would be the perfect summary of Hillary Clinton's career.

By contrast, I'm known as The Persistence. That means I

never give up. I persist in my fight for this beautiful country. And because I love this country so much, I persist in my fight for the Republican Party. But let's be real. Historically, it's not like Republicans have exactly embraced the gays. This moment we're in—this moment where the long-haired gay man in boots is hanging out with the president and the vice president in the Oval Office—is a new moment. When Donald Trump made his entrance at a rally in Greeley, Colorado, on October 30, 2016, he walked past his podium. He raised his fist in a show of power. Then he unfurled a rainbow flag that said, "LGBT for TRUMP." That was a groundbreaking moment in US history. That was a groundbreaking moment for the Republican Party. That was a groundbreaking moment for gays in America. That was a groundbreaking moment for me. That hadn't been done. Sure, maybe you had seen some Republicans here and there say they love the gays or whatever. But it was Donald Trump who showed enthusiastic and unconditional support in a very public way, support like we had never seen before.

It wasn't just campaign theatrics. Trump wasn't just trying to fit in. Back in 2000, when he was running for president, he was interviewed by the *Advocate*, an LGBT magazine. "I grew up in New York City, a town with different races, religions, and peoples. It breeds tolerance. In all truth, I don't care whether or not a person is gay. I judge people based on their capability, honesty, and merit. Being in the entertainment business—that is, owning casinos and . . . several large beauty pageants—I've worked with many gay people. I have met some tough, talented, capable, terrific people. Their lifestyle is of no interest to me." When the *Advocate* asked him if we would see gay people in his administration, he was candid. "I would want the best and brightest.

Sexual orientation would be meaningless. I'm looking for brains and experience. If the best person for the job happens to be gay, I would certainly appoint them."

That's what America First is all about. We don't care who you sleep with, as long as it's not kids, and it's consensual, and it's legal. We don't care what color you are. We don't care what religion you are. We don't care where you come from. You can come from South Africa and become an American, but you're an American first. This is about America. First. Everything else is out the window. We don't care. All of those are characteristics that have nothing to do with your actual character. At the end of the day, to quote President Trump, we want the best and the brightest. If you happen to be gay, or Black, or an atheist, or trans, it does not matter. The Democrats can pander to "marginalized communities" all they want with their empty symbolic gesturing. (Can someone please tell me why they keep adding more colors to our beautiful rainbow flag? It looks terrible!) But the polls tell the truth. Americans are sick and tired of the liberal establishment. We voted for change in 2016, 2020, and 2024. Donald J. Trump is the grand arbiter of change.

Meanwhile, the Democratic Party is just continuing on the same path that has already proven wildly unsuccessful. Listen to them right now. They're doubling down. They're tripling down. They're actually saying we haven't done enough to root out "unconscious white supremacy," "toxic masculinity," and "transphobic bigotry." In their eyes, wanting to protect your local police department's budget means you're a member of the KKK. In their eyes, a man who is ambitious and who wants to be physically strong must hate women. Through the beer goggles that have come to define the Democratic perspective, wanting your teenage daughter to compete against other teenage girls in sports means you're a virulent transphobe.

I didn't think it was possible—I really didn't—but the Democrats have become even more obsessed with identity since the 2024 election. They're now saying gay people are overrepresented among the poor. They're saying gay people face some of the highest risks of police violence. They're actually saying climate change disproportionately effects gay people. It's crazy. It's absolutely crazy what these people are saying. It makes no sense. The majority of Americans who hear this stuff, the Americans who live on Main Street, they know it's crazy. As for the gays, we know it's pandering.

Recently, I was walking down a street in Midtown Manhattan, a part of the city that is liberal, affluent, and out of touch with the rest of America to an astonishing degree. And it was the end of pride month. So, the gay stuff—it was over the top, in your face, all over the place. Stickers, T-shirts, banners, posters, flags, coffee mugs, suspenders, lanyards, sunglasses, and graffiti. Walking around, it looked like New York City had been turned into a gayer version of Provincetown. If you have ever been to P-Town, that's saying something!

The city is supportive of gay people, and that's awesome. But the ways in which these out-of-touch liberals express their support are just absolutely looney. I saw a sign that said, "Queers for Palestine." Try being a queer in Palestine. Remember twenty-five-year-old Ahmad Abu Murkhiyeh? He was a gay man who sought asylum in Israel because he feared persecution in Palestine. His decapitated torso and severed head were found on the side of the road in the West Bank. Speaking under the condition of anonymity, "M" couldn't have been clearer in his interview with the global nonprofit Fair Planet: "We, as Arab LGBT people, are viewed as trash by the Arab-Palestinian society. We are dead in their eyes." All these pro-Palestine gays and self-purported "allies" to the gay community living in Midtown Manhattan—bless their hearts!

What Americans like myself want—whether we're gay, Black, rich, poor, white, straight, Hispanic, Asian, from the Midwest, the South, or the Northeast—is an America that works for everyone. I am not a hyphenated America. I am not a "gay-American." I'm more than just what's in between my legs. I'm what's in between my ears and my ribs. My heart and my brains are what defines me—not immutable characteristics. The minority voters who came out to the polls in droves to support President Trump, they're not "African-Americans," "Hispanic-Americans," and "Asian-Americans." They're Americans—first. While the Democrats want to divide us into tribes, as they try to win elections by stoking the fires of tribalism, President Trump is trying to unite us. He understands that this isn't the Divided States of America. It's the United States of America.

Historically, this hasn't been a controversial position. Our country was founded on the idea that what unites us is more important than what divides us. When the late, great President Theodore Roosevelt delivered his speech on Americanism in 1915, he wasn't delivering a radical idea. He was delivering the idea that has made this country great:

> What is true of creed is no less true of nationality. There is no room in this country for hyphenated Americanism. When I refer to hyphenated Americans, I do not refer to naturalized Americans. Some of the very best Americans I have ever known were naturalized Americans, Americans born abroad. But a

hyphenated American is not an American at all. This is just as true of the man who puts "native" before the hyphen as of the man who puts German or Irish or English or French before the hyphen. Americanism is a matter of the spirit and of the soul. Our allegiance must be purely to the United States. We must unsparingly condemn any man who holds any other allegiance. But if he is heartily and singly loyal to this Republic, then no matter where he was born, he is just as good an American as anyone else. . . .

In my Cabinet at the time there were men of English and French, German, Irish and Dutch blood, men born on this side and men born in Germany and Scotland; but they were all Americans and nothing else; and every one of them was incapable of thinking of himself or of his fellow-countrymen, excepting in terms of American citizenship. If any one of them had anything in the nature of a dual or divided allegiance in his soul, he never would have been appointed to serve under me, and he would have been instantly removed when the discovery was made. There wasn't one of them who was capable of desiring that the policy of the United States should be shaped with reference to the interests of any foreign country or with consideration for anything, outside of the general welfare of humanity, save the honor and interest of the United States, and each was incapable of making any discrimination whatsoever among the citizens of the country he served, of our common country, save discrimination based on conduct and on conduct alone. . . .

All of us, no matter from what land our parents came, no matter in what way we may severally worship our Creator, must stand shoulder to shoulder in a united America for the elimination of race

> and religious prejudice. We must stand for a reign of equal justice to both big and small.

That is the creed of our country's founding fathers. That is President Trump's creed. That is my creed. That is the America First creed.

The Obama and Biden Years

While my viral response to the Pulse night club massacre catapulted me into the world of conservative politics—not just as a supporter, but as a leader—my commitment to the Republican Party had been longstanding. I grew up in a house where a picture of George W. Bush was taped side-by-side with Pope John Paul II to the kitchen cabinet. If you'll permit a pun, I had always been on the "right" side of history. Looking back, however, I realize the stark contrast between a globalist Republican and an America First Republican.

But it wasn't until President Barack Obama came to power that I felt a real sense of urgency regarding the direction our country was heading. To see the Democrats push through the Affordable Care Act, which most Americans, I would say, by and large, didn't want, was really just a sign of how corrupt and misguided the political landscape had become. That's why the 2010 midterm elections were such a repudiation. The Republican Party ended unified Democratic control of Congress, and they gained seats in the Senate. At the same time, the Tea Party was born.

Here I was, having just graduated from George Mason University with a 3.63 GPA—that's right, beauty and brains—and I couldn't find a job, even though I was working my behind off. Under Democratic leadership, our economy had been tanked.

For me, and countless other young Americans, the future looked like an M. Night Shyamalan film. It looked grim. Get married? Buy a home? Have kids? So many of us young people were struggling to buy groceries, pay our phone bills, and put gas in our cars. All these major life milestones for other generations, they seemed so out of reach for our generation.

When I think about my parents' generation, and even my grandparents' generation, I think about the leaders who made these milestones possible for them. When Ronald Reagan campaigned with his "Let's Make America Great Again" slogan in 1980, it foreshadowed the great movement that President Trump and JD Vance are leading now. As they know, you don't have a great country when millions of hardworking Americans feel hopeless about the future.

Obama had fed my generation a lot of talk about hope, and change, and a future where we would all make it. He promised a future where a rising tide would lift all of our boats. Do you remember his campaign speeches? Do you remember all those posters? Do you remember the fervor that was in the air? Young people—people in my generation—believed a better future was not only possible, but right on the horizon. All they had to do was get the first Black president into the White House. Well, they did get Barack Obama into the Oval Office. But the future didn't turn out the way they planned.

Here I was, a college graduate—who had done everything the hard way, the long way, and the right way—and I was picking up dog droppings (not that there's anything wrong with that). There's no shame in a hard day's work and honest labor. I also want to make it very clear that I am not a victim. While at the mercy of President Obama's botched economy, I didn't let it own me. I took my own destiny into my hands. After six months of walking dogs and seeing friends from college go on to begin careers in their fields, I decided enough was enough. So, I contacted a temporary agency and began doing jobs for Alexandria City Public Schools. After doing some work at TC Williams High School, I ended up doing long-term work for William Ramsay Elementary School. They say that every job you perform in life ultimately sets you up for your next one. This couldn't be more true of working for the public school system in Northern Virginia. With eight hundred students, from pre-K through fifth grade, 1,600 moms and dads, dozens of staff, and a diverse community that was 70 percent Hispanic, I learned a lot about service from working in the main office. I was so dedicated to my job that I even learned Spanish to be able to speak to our families and studied Arabic in my free time to welcome the incoming refugee families. After working a full-time job at the school, I would spend the afternoon walking dogs. While I clearly wasn't afraid of hard work, I knew there was more for me in this world. And I also knew that there are presidents who create opportunities for hardworking Americans—and there are presidents who stifle them.

My story represented the stories of young Americans across the country. It didn't matter if you went to UCLA, Ole Miss, or the University of Florida, we were all struggling across the board. Crippled by student debt and confronted with an economy that was no longer working for everyone, President Obama's radical promise of change had been a total sham. The only people who seemed to benefit from his administration were the Wall Street bankers who paid for his campaign.

The Obama administration made so many terrible decisions that it's difficult to find a place to even begin. Under his leadership, the border had basically ceased to exist. If you were looking at America from another country, the message was clear: come here illegally, steal someone's job, get free health insurance, vote six times in the election, Laken Riley someone, and rest assured that you won't get deported. During the Obama years, criminal illegal aliens were flooding our country faster than MSNBC tried to kill stories about Hunter Biden's laptop. And if you're an illegal alien who wants to go to college for free, you can rest assured that Harvard, Yale, and the other elite universities will welcome you with open arms. They'll even pay you to come! You're a lot more valuable to their DEI agenda—and the minority-laden photographs they have on their institution's website—than a white student who did things the hard way, the long way, and the right way. NYU would rather admit Michelle Jones, a Black woman who murdered her son, than a working-class white kid from the rural South who never committed a crime in his life. Any liberal who is even remotely confused by the widespread distrust of and disdain for America's universities, especially the Ivy League, is as out of touch with reality as Sleepy Joe Biden during his last term in office.

Growing up, I was into *Lord of the Rings* and *Star Wars*. These are epic films that are political to a certain extent. You have the Fellowship versus Mordor. You have the Rebel Alliance waging war against the Galactic Empire. There are heroes who are fighting for the good of all—waging a war of truth, of courage, and of benevolence. Their war isn't guided by the compass of greed. It's guided by the compass of compassion. On the flipside, you have the villains. They want to conquer and destroy. They see nothing beyond their own interests. Benevolence is not in their vocabulary. They are nefarious. They are malicious. They are wicked. They are the serpent in the Garden of Eden.

Lord of the Rings was shaped by Christianity. *Star Wars* was shaped by Christianity. These stories are so powerful because they're so perennial. While the CGI is new, the basic plot points are as old as time itself. Evil is real. It manifests in our hearts, our minds, and our souls. But good is also real. There are heroes who emerge to vanquish the evil. Sometimes they carry swords and shields. Other times they carry colonial-era muskets. In the more fantastical adaptations, they carry wizard staffs and lightsabers. But the core is perennial. There's always this light and this dark, this yin and this yang, and this good versus evil.

I grew up Catholic. I believe evil exists. I can't read the minds of Barack Obama, Hillary Clinton, and Kamala Harris. I'm not in Elizabeth Warren's head. I'm not in Bernie Sanders's head either. But one thing I will never understand for as long as I live is how, how could anybody, how could any Democrat be for open borders? Knowing the crimes that criminal illegal aliens have committed, knowing that fentanyl is coming into our country, killing three hundred Americans a day, knowing that women and children are getting raped because of our open border. How could anyone with a moral compass that isn't totally smashed to pieces want to get rid of our borders? When you are fully capable of mitigating human suffering, when you are fully capable of alleviating it—of outright stopping it—but you are instead encouraging it, and using your power to escalate it, how is that not evil?

This is the America I saw with President Obama at the helm. As criminal illegal aliens were remaking our beautiful country in their decrepit image, the Democrats, especially those standing alongside Crazy Bernie, wanted to increase the corporate tax. Are any of these people familiar with the most basic principles of economic thought? Have any of these people ever read a single history textbook, a basic primer on the free market, or the latest issue of any reputable business journal? Those kinds of tax increases have only pushed businesses out of America and into the arms of China and our other enemies. There is nothing sane about sending our important job creators to other countries. It is suicidal economics. And it has had terrible downstream effects for all the young people who are now struggling to provide for themselves and their families.

So, there I was, struggling to get a job in my field, and the Democrats were working day and night to ensure that young people like me would have even fewer options for employment. There's nothing wrong with being a dog walker. It's respectable work that provides an important service to people. But to be candid, I didn't work my behind off for four years to pick up dog droppings for the rest of my life. As I said, I have always been a Republican. However, the Obama administration really made me cognizant of the harm that the Democratic Party was doing to this country. A lot of that harm wasn't just affecting me; it was going to affect future generations. If people in my generation couldn't get jobs—and because they couldn't get jobs, they were not going to have children and grandchildren—could you imagine what the future of this country was going to look like?

There are multiple reasons why birth rates in the United States have been declining rapidly. But one piece of that story is the fact that people my age—quite literally—cannot afford to have kids. Another reason is the degrading of the nuclear family. While the Republicans are telling Americans to procreate and to produce loving families, the Democrats are telling people that families don't matter, that women shouldn't have kids, and that it's "internalized sexism" for women to believe otherwise. Women are constantly being told that a fulfilling life isn't lived at home. It's lived in the workplace. Any man who disagrees is "oppressive" and part of "the patriarchy."

That was the whole messaging of Hillary Clinton's "Pantsuit Nation." Men are malicious. Marriage is slavery. Children are oppressive. Families are evil. Pantsuits—a symbol of corporate femininity—are holy. From their perspective, it's the morally virtuous path to abandon men, marriage, children, and even families. As the title of a *Vice* article puts it, "We Can't Have a Feminist Future Without Abolishing the Family." They're not alone. Left-wing *Current Affairs* magazine ran an article titled, "Why We Should Abolish the Family." Verso, the leading left-wing activist press in the world, even published a manifesto, *Abolish the Family: A Manifesto for Care and Liberation*. This isn't a *Babylon Bee* book. This isn't satire. This is real left-wing thinking.

"Maybe AOC hasn't found the right person," remarked Vice President JD Vance. "Whatever the case may be, AOC has said basically—if you look at her public remarks on this—that it's immoral to have children because of climate change concerns. Right? This is, let's just be direct, a sociopathic attitude towards family." As the vice president also explained, and I agree with him completely, "It's one thing to have a society where some people don't have kids. It's another thing to build an entire political movement that is explicitly anti-child and anti-family. And that's what the Left in this country is. It is anti-child and anti-family.

"What does it say about our civilization that so many of our leaders don't have kids? What does it say about the incentives that are built into the Democrats' entire movement that they reward the young people who don't have families instead of the young people who do?" As our vice president put it, "I think it's just pretty sick . . . and it suggests something pretty broken." He is absolutely right. Yet, because of the Left's war on reality, and its Orwellian language games, it's people who want to have kids who are now being treated as sociopaths. They're being treated as the people who don't care about planet Earth, and women's rights, and so on.

Online, you see women shamed for wanting to stay at home and be mothers. It's disgusting. It's also what's given birth to the "trad wife" movement. These are women who aren't going to keep quiet because the liberals want to cancel them for having kids. These are women who take pride in the monumental challenges and joys of motherhood. These are women who aren't going to have an abortion just because the Democrats have made it legal. These are the women who are making our country great again. These are also the women who were left behind by the Democratic Party.

On the eve of the November 2024 election, a young woman went viral for sharing how she felt: "I would love to be able to live on a homestead and go milk my cow and take the eggs out of the chicken coop, and have one baby in the belly and one on my hip, and another toddler behind me. That's like my dream, but I can't (expletive) do that because the way the economy is set up is I'm forced to work. I'm forced to get an education, a higher education, a college degree, in order to make enough money. . . . Being a single working woman absolutely sucks. . . . I would go back to the 1950s in a second just so I wouldn't have to deal with this."

As the Democrats bring more criminal illegal aliens to our country, we're now facing a population crisis with our own native-born citizens, the people who make this country great. "For a population to remain stable—flat, no growth, no decline—women, on average, have to have 2.1 kids," reflects a recent report, "In the U.S., that number is 1.6, and dropping." If there is a better definition of national suicide, I am not aware of it. From their border policies to their extremist ideas about marriage, and families, and domestic life, it is almost as if the Democrats' sole purpose is to the destroy the United States of America.

When I talk about the threats posed by the Democratic Party to the United States of America, I am literally talking about existential threats.

This is the kind of evil I expect to see when I watch *The Fellowship of the Ring*. It's what I expect from *The Empire Strikes Back*—remember, the dark emperor was a senator. It's what I expect when I read Genesis. It's not what I should expect—what anyone in this country should expect—from one of our two political parties. Given the nature of the historical moment we are living through, I don't think it was a coincidence that the Tea Party, and later Trumpism, emerged when it did. These were responses to a question that was provoked by the Obama administration: Why was the Democratic Party pushing so many America Last policies?

While President Obama spearheaded the America Last agenda, President Biden continued to bring it to fruition. "Thus far in Fiscal Year 2024, with only four full months completed, nearly a million illegal aliens have crossed the southern border," reflected *Breitbart* journalist John Binder back on February 2, 2024. "In Fiscal Year 2022, Biden broke records by overseeing close to 2.37 million illegal aliens at the border, and he shattered that record the following fiscal year when 2.47 million arrived. For perspective, about 3.6 million Americans are born each year. Thus, two years of American births are equivalent to the total number of illegal border crossings Biden has overseen." The Great Placement isn't a "theory." It's the reality of Democratic policies.

When I see lawn signs that say, "No One is Illegal," I can't help but think of all the Americans who have lost jobs and who have seen their wages driven down because of those Democratic policies. And how could Democrats possibly even say they are pro-union when they are allowing illegal aliens to take union jobs that should be going to American workers? Every policy and every word coming out of their mouths is dripping with hypocrisy. It's truly Orwellian the way the Democrats have used their language games to create the now widespread belief that moral people need to be against borders. This was the propaganda of President Obama, later picked up by President Biden. It's the propaganda that they poured into the colleges and universities back when I was a student—and that they continue to pour into the colleges and universities today. It's propaganda, plain and simple, because it isn't true. It's propaganda because it's serving an agenda.

I think there are many reasons for the suicidal policies of the Democrats—policies that put Americans last—but one thing is certain: their policies drive down wages. Steve Bannon hit the nail on the head in a recent interview with Russell Brand. He talked about why these elites want to flood our country with illegal criminal aliens. "They're very open about why they want so many migrants into the country—we call them illegal alien invaders—it's to drive down the wages of working-class African Americans and Hispanics. . . . Now, if you look at our budgets and all these massive deficits, they have baked in ten million illegal alien invaders into the permanent economic model of the United

States because they understand that this will drive down wages." As Bannon correctly observes, "the only people that get hurt are the people farthest down the chain."

Another thing is also certain: When Democrats bring criminal illegal aliens into this country, those criminals are counted in the United States Census. That allows Democrats to gain more seats in the House of Representatives. They've been using this same playbook for decades, and it has paid off in major ways. The Democratic Party gains political power by encouraging illegal and unlawful action to occur. Because of their blatant disregard for the law, they get more votes. That's what all of this comes down to: votes, votes, and more votes. Notwithstanding all their political bunkum about how much they love immigrants from Mexico and other countries, the truth is much different. They love votes. That the Democrats are willing to use bodies, and use people, and allow terrible things to happen for their own political prowess—I don't know what other word I can use to describe it: It's evil.

About forty-five miles east of Manhattan, Kayla Cuevas and Nisa Mickens turned up dead. They were sixteen and fifteen. They had been beaten to death with baseball bats and machetes. Who murdered these young girls in cold blood? Members of MS-13, a gang founded by Salvadorian immigrants that has been terrorizing Americans since the 1980s. Suffolk County, were the girls were found, has been described by the *New York Times* as a "hot spot" for MS-13. This is a neighborhood in New York, not a favela in South America. New Yorkers shouldn't have to live in fear of being hacked to death by criminal illegal aliens. They shouldn't have to worry every time their daughters walk home from school. After Kayla's gruesome murder, who did her mother Evelyn turn to? She had a meeting with Donald Trump. She also attended the

State of the Union address as his guest. How many teenage girls like Kayla and Nisa would still be alive if the Democrats took our borders seriously? How many would still be alive if they had put American lives first?

The funny thing is that the people who are supposedly supposed to be most sympathetic to the Democrats' push for open borders—our beautiful Mexicans, and Venezuelans, and other folks—hate open borders. According to *Axios*, "the percentage of Latinos who say they support building a border wall and deporting all undocumented immigrants has jumped by at least 10 points since 2021." Of course, if you're a tenured professor at the University of California, Los Angeles, living inside a gated community in Santa Monica, you don't have to worry about an illegal alien stealing your job for lower wages and hacking your daughters to death. But if you're the Mexican American who came here legally, who is cleaning the college classrooms, and who takes the bus home every night to a run-down apartment in Skid Row, you do. Yet, the Democrats constantly give the impression that the "Latinx" population—whatever that made-up term is supposed to mean—love them and their policies. According to the Pew Research Center, just one in four US Hispanics have even heard of that term. Just three percent use it.

By the same token, Democrats say they love Black people. They'll put up their fist and they'll scream Black lives matter until their voice is hoarse and they are blue in the face. Moreover, they'll shame you to death if you don't shout it with them. Well, number one, I want to say that Black lives do matter—but not in the way that expression is normally used. When I say Black lives matter, I'm really talking about American lives mattering. Whether you're a Democrat or a Republican, we should all be putting

Black Americans, and brown Americans, and white Americans—all Americans—above criminal illegal aliens. The facts speak for themselves. There are 3.6 million Black children living in poverty. Dear Nancy Pelosi: if you care about Black people so much, why are you financing, resourcing, and helping criminal illegal aliens over the millions of Black children who are living in poverty and dodging used needles on the streets in your city and the rest of this country? Furthermore, where were the Black Lives Matter protests for Kayla and Nisa? Oh, right, there were none. They weren't murdered by a conservative or the police, so their deaths couldn't be used as political tools to attack Republicans. It wasn't the correct type of murder. Black lives don't matter to Democrats unless it results in securing more power for their party.

Back in 2020, when I was out in San Francisco picking up trash in dying parts of that city, I never bumped into Representative Pelosi. I assume she was hanging out at her vineyard, which the *Los Angeles Times* said makes her the fourth richest Californian in Congress. Or maybe she was hanging out at her house in Pacific Heights, which *Politico* describes as "one of the ritziest sections of one of the wealthiest cities in America." Regardless of where she was, she wasn't out in the streets with my team and me to clean up trash in her own city. There's a video from our time there that went viral with fifty million views. In it, I'm talking to a group of people who had stopped to see what we were up to. "Why are illegal immigrants more important than Americans?" "Why are illegal immigrants more important than homeless people sleeping on the streets?" "Why do we, and one of the biggest economies here in California, take care of illegal immigrants, but our people are sleeping on the streets?" If Nancy Pelosi is reading this book, I'd still like to hear an answer to that.

Tucker Carlson went viral after he made a similar speech at Turning Point USA's Student Action Summit on July 11, 2025. Like President Trump, Tucker was blunt and to the point:

> I'll tell you what it is. It's the frustration of normal people watching a certain class of people get away with everything, every single time. That's what it is and that drives me absolutely bonkers. By the way, it's one of the things that bothers me about immigration. As someone who got arrested in Syracuse, New York, as a kid because I had an expired driver's license, and brought to a cell. I'm watching people come . . . That actually happened. I have done time. It does change a man. Yes, I joined a gang. But I watch sixty million people come into the country illegally or overstay their fake refugee status or whatever. And the whole thing's a scam. And they get housing vouchers and free education and free cell phones and plane tickets. It's like, wait a second. Not only are they not getting punished for breaking American law, as I would and have, they're getting rewarded for it. The unfairness of it drives you crazy.

More recently, I visited a place that was largely held by the Black community, and they were celebrating President Trump, trying to stop birthright citizenship, and they see themselves as freedmen. Men, that's how they identified, and that's what they wanted President Trump to know about them. F-R-E-E-D-M-E-N. A freedman isn't the same as an African American. They are Black Americans. They are descendants of freedmen, not Africa. They are first and foremost proud Americans. In a similar vein, the beautiful gay conservatives who turned #GaysForTrump into a viral moment are first and foremost proud Americans. Under

President Obama, anti-patriotism was at an all-time high. That was when NFL quarterback Colin Kaepernick, a role model for kids of all colors, but especially Black kids, refused to stand for our beautiful national anthem. In this Humpty Dumpty world, it is our brave police officers and military men and women—not violent MS-13 gang members—who are the targets of liberal vitriol. It is our proud Americans who are looked down upon as nothing more than a "basket of deplorables."

It's not right. It's not right that Americans—including the African Americans who don't share Kaepernick's hatred for our country—are afraid to express their dissent for the liberal agenda in public. Recently, I was at a Starbucks. When I'm out in public like this, I'm still thinking about how I can initiate conversations and get out the vote. What I love to do, I love to wear a T-shirt, and I love to have stickers on the back of my laptop, that show people where I stand. I'll be sipping my caramel macchiato in a T-shirt that says, "I'm Gay and Voting for Trump." Or I'll be working on my laptop, and I'll have a sticker that says, in big, beautiful rainbow letters, "Gays for Trump." Sometimes I'll just write a statement on a piece of paper and tape it to the back of my computer. "I'm Gay and Democrats Don't Own Me." It's very grassroots. And, frankly, especially when you're in a liberal echo chamber like Manhattan or San Francisco, it's fun to be a little bit provocative. But I'm not a provocateur. I don't talk to anybody unless they talk to me first. But I'm mindful of where I sit. I'll be sitting by the door, facing the front, so every person who walks in to get a Mint Majesty tea, or coffee, they'll see me.

This particular day, a Black man walks walked into Starbucks. He sees the back of my computer. He's like, "Hey man, that's so cool. I love Trump!" I'm like, "That's awesome! Are you registered to vote at your current address?" This man ends up sitting down at my table, and we end up having a great conversation. He was just such a friendly guy. But what I remember most was what he said once we really started talking. "You're so brave," he tells me, "I have a Trump hat in my car, but I'm worried to wear it, I'm afraid to wear it." I tell him, "Go get your hat. You need to wear that hat more often. We can't allow people to shame us into acting differently. We can't allow people to pressure us into not being our true selves." Five decades after the Stonewall Riots, I was talking to an American who was still afraid to come out of the closet. This wasn't the gay closet. This was the political closet.

So this man goes to his car. He walks back into Starbucks in his Make America Great Again hat. It is red. It is bright. It is beautiful. We continue talking. We continue having a great conversation. I'm learning from him. He's learning from me. This relates back to what I am constantly talking about with the power of one person to make a difference. Then this white woman walks in. She gives us a look. After she orders her drink, she walks over to our table. She looks at my new friend, this Black gentleman, and says, "Are you really wearing that hat?" It was the same tone of voice that Hillary Clinton had used when she referred to millions of Americans as deplorables. This man, who had nothing but friendliness in his voice, kindly responds, "Yeah, I support Trump." But me, I was more defensive. I'm like, "Why do you look at the Black guy and ask him that question when we're both sitting here together? Why are you going after him?" It was like this Black man had run away from the liberal plantation. Here he was, a free man trying to enjoy a coffee in Starbucks, and this white woman was infuriated.

She loses it. She turns into a raging bull—triggered by that red hat—who wants to drive her liberal horns through our hearts. I'm a millennial activist. I use social media to my advantage. So I take out my phone. I'm not recording her face because it's important to be kind, even when faced with gross ignorance. But I'm interested in the truth. And the truth of this interaction was the truth of why so many minorities want nothing to do with the Democratic Party. The video is on social media. You can watch it for yourself. You can hear her rant. You can listen to her accost a gay guy and a Black guy because they don't want to vote for her crooked politicians. At the end, a police officer in Starbucks had to escort this crazy liberal outside. The baristas come over to ask us if we're okay. The video, which has been seen by thousands of people, exemplifies what many of us gays, and Blacks, and minorities had known for years: the Left isn't as tolerant as they say they are.

Isn't that what cancel culture is all about? If you disagree, or even if you don't express sufficient enthusiasm for liberal positions, they will cancel you. They will come after your business. They will come after your kids. And they will not stop until you have a proverbial scarlet letter branded into your skin. Do you still read Harry Potter to your kids? If so, you're a transphobe. Do you watch Fox News at night? Then you must be a racist. The rhetorical arms race being waged by the Democrats—Kamala Harris called Trump a "fascist," Alexandria Ocasio-Cortez proclaimed that "this is fascism at our door," and Elizabeth "Pocahontas" Warren said, "every day that goes by, Donald Trump is making our nation look more and more like a fascist state"—isn't just hyperbolic. It's filled with as much nonsense as a scene in *Alice in Wonderland*. But it's buttressed by a punitive enforcement mechanism—mainstream America calls it cancel culture—that never sleeps.

Cancel culture is different than accountability culture. The latter rightfully holds people accountable. For example, it was right to hold progressives who celebrated Charlie Kirk's assassination accountable. There is an important and distinct difference between disagreeing with someone's viewpoint and openly praising political murder. Charlie Kirk—by using the tools of debate, not violence—was challenging cancel culture. The coward who ended his life instead chose to use a tool of violence. That should not be cause for celebration.

I'm a data guy. I love data. I look at data every week when I'm strategizing with my team about our next move. According to a recent Hill-Harris X poll, "seventy-one percent of registered voters said they strongly or somewhat believe that cancel culture has gone too far." According to the Foundation for Individual Rights and Expression, "nearly 6 in 10 Americans feel that our nation's democracy is threatened because people are afraid to voice their opinions." Even Harvard, which isn't exactly a bastion of free speech, corroborated this data. In a Harvard CAPS-Harris Poll survey, "sixty-four percent of respondents said that there is 'a growing cancel culture' that is a threat to their freedom."

When President Donald Trump shouts "let's grid of PC!" he's not only connecting with his base. He's connecting with the growing number of Americans who are sick and tired of the witch hunts being waged in the name of the Democratic Party. Moreover, Trump personifies an authenticity that we have not seen since Ronald Reagan called the Soviet Union "the evil empire." Reagan's campaign slogan was Make America Great. It's not a coincidence that Trump's is Make America Great Again. It takes outsiders to come in and shake up the system. It took Donald

Trump entering the realm of politics for Americans to understand how broken and how corrupt our country has become. You can't shake up the system by playing by the preexisting rules. Instead of playing nice with the Democrats and the Republicans, Trump was willing to say things that politicians on both sides of the aisle would never say.

Some of these politicians have nefarious motives. Others just want to play nice. Nobody wants to be the one to say, "We need to kick all of these criminal illegal aliens the heck out of our country." When Donald Trump is in power, there's no baloney. There's no delays. There's no wishy-washy rhetoric. President Trump doesn't wear the kid gloves. He gets down to business. He's a man of action. "Oh, but wait, these undocumented immigrants came here for a better life!" Of course they did! The United States is the best country in the world. That's why people are flooding our borders. But that doesn't mean we have to let them in. It certainly doesn't mean we have to let them stay. It can be simultaneously true that these people come from worse countries, that their lives would be better in our country, and that we don't have a place for them here. These are the sorts of hard truths that Democrats, and even some Republicans, are unwilling to talk about. President Trump doesn't just talk the talk; he walks the walk.

If Trump had not taken the Oval Office, these politicians would continue to kick the can down the road. The D.C. class is made up of people who go along to get along. "Sure, we'll give Iran $1.7 million if they pinky promise they're not going to build nukes." Does anyone really think that Hillary Clinton, Joe Biden, or Kamala Harris would have bombed Iran's nuclear facilities? It's easier to imagine the end of the world—quite literally—than a Democratic president who is capable of taking decisive action like

Donald Trump. If Comrade Kamala had been elected to office, I imagine she would have extended her hand to Ali Hosseini Khamenei, the supreme leader of Iran. "Can you please come to the table? I will promise you an amazing deal like the one Obama gave you." This is a vice president who said she would not have done anything different than President Joe Biden, a man whose unparalleled cognitive deficiencies were publicly broadcasted for four straight years—not just to his own people, but to our adversaries abroad. If Kamala were president, billions of dollars of cash would be wrapped with a beautiful red bow and on the way to the Ayatollah as they chant, "Death to America!"

In politics, people just become so accustomed to being nice, to saying the right thing, and to not rocking the boat. Before Trump, it was more important to say the politically correct thing—"Iran is our friend," "It's Islamophobic to stop their production of nuclear energy," "Don't call them Muslim terrorists"—than the correct thing. No, America is not safe when our enemies have nuclear weapons. No, we cannot have a country when our borders cease to exist. No, we cannot afford a "universal basic income." No, our taxpayer money shouldn't be going to NGOs trying to slay the largely mythical dragons of racism and climate change. No, men cannot participate in women's sports. No, we shouldn't hire people based on their race. No, we shouldn't defund the police. No, Joseph Stalin was not a great man.

While the issues are different, they are all part and parcel of both liberal cancel culture and the swamp in Washington, D.C. In 2016, 2020, and 2024, tens of millions of American voted to drain the swamp.

The Rise of the Persistence

In 2014, I was done. I wanted to make our country great again. As opposed to pointing the finger at other people and asking, "What are you going to do about it?" I pointed the finger back at myself and asked, "What am I going to do about it?" Be the change you want to see in the world. I know it's cliché, and it's hackneyed, and maybe it's even a little bit sentimental, but back when President Barack Hussein Obama was catapulting our country down the grim path of communism, I really believed I could make a difference. I really believed that I didn't need to be Elon Musk. I didn't need to be President Trump. I didn't even need other people to back me up. I just needed to get to work. Imagine if 330 million Americans actively sought to implement positive, constructive changes in this country? We could transform the United States, as well as the rest of the world, for the better. I believed all of this back then, and I still believe it in my heart to this day.

A lot of gays get stereotyped as powerless because there are members of our community who love to paint themselves as helpless victims. Thanks Pete Buttigieg and Ellen DeGeneres! But I'm not a victim. I'm a 100-percent, USDA-certified, Type-A alpha male down to my bones. That means you take charge. Quincy Jones used to say, "no paralysis through analysis!" In other words, you have to be decisive in life. That's especially true in the world of grassroots politics. Sure, I will analyze all the moves on the chessboard. As I said, I'm constantly looking at data, talking to my team, and otherwise taking in all the information I need to make the best decisions possible. But I don't hesitate to make a decision. I don't hesitate to take action. I won't wait for somebody else to make the first move. I certainly won't wait for my opponents to make the first move. That Nike mantra has always resonated with me: just do it. How do we get from point A to point Z? What concrete steps do we have to take? How do we increase our wins and reduce our losses? "Leaders, true leaders," says President Trump, "take responsibility for the success of the team, and understand that they must also take responsibility for the failure." I naturally fell into a leadership role because, to be perfectly honest, a lot of people in this country aren't ready to lead.

That year, and with a fire lit under my behind, I packed all my clothes into boxes, I filled my gas tank, and I moved to Texas. The next year, with my help, Greg Abbott was elected governor of the Lone Star State. It was a huge win, and Governor Abbott won again in 2018, and again in 2022. In the words of President Trump:

> Greg Abbott is a fighter and a Great Governor for the incredible people of Texas. No Governor has done more to secure the Border and keep our communities safe than Governor Abbott. Greg is a staunch defender of the Second Amendment and has made Texas a Second Amendment Sanctuary State. Texas has become a job-creating machine, and our partnership helped restore America's economic power and success. Greg is also very tough on crime, fully supports the brave men and women of Law Enforcement, and is all in on Election Integrity. Governor Greg Abbott will continue to be a great leader for the Lone Star State, and has my Complete and Total Endorsement for re-election. He will never let you down!

Reading that endorsement from President Trump makes me proud to have helped Greg Abbott get into office. That said, I made the right decision to leave Texas. The presidential election was on the horizon, and I knew that I could better serve the Republican Party elsewhere. Texas wasn't going to vote for Hillary Clinton. It was going to vote for Donald Trump. So it didn't make sense for me to stick around. I wanted to be on the ground connecting with Americans in a swing state. Serendipitously, I got a call from the Republican Party of Virginia. "Scott," they said, "we need you up here in Virginia. We need you up here to campaign for Donald J. Trump." Virginia has thirteen Electoral College votes. I thought to myself, if we win Virginia, there is no way the Democrats are going to take the Oval Office. Without a second thought, I packed all my clothes back into boxes, I filled my gas tank, and I made the move to the Mother of States.

Virginia, that was my first leadership role. I had several staff below me, and we campaigned night and day for Republican presidential candidate Donald Trump. In that role, I learned a lot more about the importance of primaries. By way of example, the second congressional district is a swing House seat there. It's a House seat that flips back and forth between blue and red. It's an area that's up for grabs. This was a period when Republican Scott Taylor, a former Navy SEAL, was running for office. In those kinds of races, you learn a tremendous amount about different voting blocs and the importance of different areas. In that area of Virginia, you have the largest Naval base in the world. In Manhattan, it doesn't matter if a candidate has served in the Navy. In Norfolk, Virginia, it matters a whole lot.

I went all out in Virginia. It didn't matter if my team and I were talking to people downtown or on a university campus, we got to work registering voters. We had the first Republican booth at the pride celebration in Virginia Beach. We had one big, beautiful flag for everyone to see. That flag had the real rainbow—not the weird rainbow. As we registered voters, it was just those gorgeous red, orange, yellow, green, blue, and purple stripes stacked on top of each other and blowing in the ocean breeze. There was no brown stripe, circle, or arrow. Our flag said, "Republicans Love You" in big, black, bold letters. We didn't have any problems. In fact, we had a number of gays come to our table to tell us they loved us too. At one point, a drag queen posted up at our table. As I looked around, thinking about where the Republican Party had been, where it was now, and where it was heading under the leadership of Donald Trump, it was hard not to be moved. It really was a phenomenal moment in history.

Helping the Republican Party of Virginia helped me become a better leader—not just a leader who gets the job done, but a leader who my team appreciates, who my team looks up to, and who my team constantly aspires to emulate. Effective grassroots political leadership can't be taught in a field manual or in a TikTok video. It most certainly can't be taught on a college campus. It really is a boots-on-the-ground education alongside real people who have real personalities, real strengths, and real weaknesses. There are so many examples of what that de facto education in leadership entails. But a big part of it is meeting your teammates where they are. It's learning how to create a supportive and non-toxic work environment where they feel valued. I know if I motivate my staff, and I keep my staff happy and excited about the work they're doing, they will be more effective in our office and in the field. Moreover, they will trust me, and they will stand with me until the end. In this political game, loyalty is everything.

One of my staff back in Virginia, she was married to a Navy SEAL. He was out on duty. She said, "Scott, my husband is going to be in Florida. Can I go down to Florida?" Granted, we were explicitly told, "Do not leave Virginia." The rules could not have been clearer. But guess what? I'm not leading a college campus. I'm not running an HR department in Silicon Valley. I'm not here to dot my I's and cross my T's so that everything looks good on paper when I have my weekly meeting with the bureaucrat above me, and he has his weekly meeting with the bureaucrat above him, and he has his weekly meeting with the bureaucrat above him. That's not the world I live in.

I live in the world of grassroots politics. If there's a rule I'm expected to follow, it better serve the only goal that matters to me: political victory. In this world, sometimes you need to bend the rules a little bit. This is a world where people aren't getting big salaries and long vacations. They're in it because their hearts are in it. So you better take care of them. I told this woman who was married to one of our great servicemen, "As long as you finish your work, get your numbers in, hit your voter registrations, hit your doors, do what you have to do, you can go to Florida. Enjoy the weekend. Be with your husband. He's an American hero. Nobody has to know. My lips are sealed."

That's how you lead.

That how you keep people loyal to you.

That's how you run a grassroots political movement.

That's how you achieve political victories.

There's a book called *The Obstacle Is the Way* by Ryan Holiday. In it, Holiday quotes Andy Grover, the former CEO of Intel: "Bad companies are destroyed by crisis. Good companies survive them. Great companies are improved by them." It's the same thing with these interpersonal challenges that constantly arise in the world of grassroots politics. I knew the rules. I knew I was supposed to follow them. I could have told her "No. These are the rules. You can't bend the rules!" I could have denied her request to see her husband. I could have faced this challenge that way I was told to face it. I could have stuck to the rulebook I was given. And guess what? I could have very well lost this woman's support.

To be perfectly honest, I knew better. I know that some rules are meant to followed, and some rules are—in certain contexts—meant to be broken. I didn't see the point. So I turned a challenge into a win. She would have understandably been upset if she could not see her husband. But because of the way I responded to this challenge—this obstacle—not only was our relationship not jeopardized, it was actually strengthened. "All great victories, be they in politics, business, art, or seduction," writes Holiday, "involved resolving vexing problems with a potent cocktail of creativity, focus, and daring." It was in Virginia that I learned how to be the leader who embraces all challenges—no matter how big, small, inconsequential, or absolutely decisive—as opportunities.

In *The Art of the Deal*, President Trump writes: "In my life, there are two things I've found I'm very good at: overcoming obstacles and motivating good people to do their best work. One of the challenges ahead is how to use those skills as successfully in the service of others as I've done, up to now, on my own behalf." I feel the same about my work as a grassroots political activist. I aspire to overcome obstacles and to motivate the good people I work with every day to do their absolute best work every day. I also aspire to serve others. I'm grateful that President Trump is back in the Oval Office for ten million reasons and more. But one of those reasons is more personal than others: I, once again, have a president who I can look to for inspiration, one who inspires me to do my very best work—in the service of others—every day.

Like Donald Trump, I'm less interested in doing things the

way they have always been done. I think red tape is made for cutting. I'm more interested in doing things the effective way. When I had that viral moment in San Francisco—a once great city that has devolved into San Fransicko, to use journalist Michael Shellenberger's words, because of the Democratic Party—it's because I had chosen to do things differently. When I had my first truly viral moment after the Pulse night club shooting, it was because I had chosen to do things differently. The America First movement isn't here simply to recreate what has worked well in the past. I grew up with George W. Bush in my kitchen. But the neoconservative movement had its limits. The America First movement has no limits.

Obviously, I love my beautiful Republicans. But, like President Trump, I'm not afraid to call a spade a spade. For years, the Republican Party had not shown up for the gay community. For so long, the gay community had voted for Democrats. A big part of that problem was the messaging that came from the Right. It simply wasn't the kind of messaging that made gay Americans feel seen. It wasn't the kind of messaging that made gay Americans feel welcomed. When I tweeted that big, beautiful hashtag—#GaysForTrump—I wasn't following a script handed down to me from the Republican National Convention. I was being spontaneous. I was being my authentic self. I was coming out of the closet. I was showing up for my gay brothers and sisters, many of whom were growing increasingly disenchanted by the party that had claimed them for decades. And guess what? I wasn't alone.

From Texas, to Virginia, to my current work in Pennsylvania, people are frequently perplexed by my ability to connect with folks from all walks of life. They say, "Scott, how do I get the Black community's vote?" "Scott, how do I earn Asian votes?"

"Scott, how do I get the Amish to show up at the polls? They don't even own cars!" Well, I want to make it clear, I've had success with the Black community, the Asian community, and the Amish community. I'm not Black. I'm not Asian. I'm not Amish. I don't have a Shenandoah. I don't make my own cheese. I don't ride a horse and buggy. If you asked me how to draw water from a well, I would have to ask ChatGPT.

What I do isn't the result of decades studying political science at Harvard, Yale, or Cornell. It's not easy—in fact, it's often not easy—but it isn't complicated. It's simple. I show up. I show up again. And I keep showing up. Whether it's an Amish farm or Chinatown, it doesn't matter. I show up. I shut my mouth. I open my ears. I listen. And when a stranger is done explaining, or ranting, or screaming, I ask them questions. I'm an active listener. I show them that I've been listening to their stories, their hopes, their dreams, and their concerns. Politics is for using power to create positive action, and there is great power in the act of listening.

This is something our president knows well. It doesn't matter if you're the vice president, the landscaper at the golf course, or a grassroots political activist trying to reclaim Pennsylvania for the Republican Party, President Trump wants to hear what you think—even if he might disagree with what you think. In the words of Secretary of Education Linda McMahon, who has known the president for more than twenty years, "he really focuses on what he's doing and really cares about what he's doing," and "he is a really good listener." Or as Karoline Leavitt, our 36th White House Press Secretary, described the president, "The best thing about him that I've learned is he's a great listener. And he values the opinions of everybody in the room." As Secretary Leavitt explains, "He'll be talking about tariffs, and he'll ask somebody in the room who he knows, and who everybody knows, has no experience in the world of tariffs, but he genuinely wants to hear the opinions of everybody else before he makes a decision."

That's leadership in action.

That's the power of listening.

That's the kind of leadership and listening I aspire to emulate in my own work.

From the Oval Office to the frontlines where my team and I are working to Make America Great Again every single day, this is what the America First movement is all about.

From the landscaper to the server taking your order at the local restaurant, this movement is all about listening to the beautiful Americans who make our country great.

It's all about putting them—and their needs, and their hopes, and their visions for the future of this country—first.

As the next chapter reveals, I was listening when Donald Trump called our once great city of Baltimore "a disgusting, rat and rodent infested mess." I was listening when the people of Baltimore—on the Right, on the Left, and in the center—asked for help. Above all, I was listening when my team and I headed to the east coast to make Baltimore great again.

Chapter 2

THE BALTIMORE CLEANUP

Back in 2019, President Trump started sharing photos of the trash in Baltimore, Maryland. These weren't photos of crushed soda cans on a sidewalk or a plastic bag blowing in the wind. These were photos of rats. Not the Democratic politicians who run that city. These weren't liberal rats. These were literal rats. Big, chunky, ferocious rats. Some of them were big enough to snatch a child off the streets. I'm exaggerating, but only a little bit. The Democratic establishment had left Baltimore behind.

At the time, Trump was resharing material from Kimberly Klacik. Kim is a businesswoman, a political commentator, and a former congressional candidate from Maryland's 7th congressional district. She grew up in Maryland. She still calls Baltimore County home. And she was sick and tired of seeing what this once great American city had turned into.

Kim, who is a beautiful Black woman, isn't someone who is fooled by the Democratic Party's purported commitment to people like her. In a video seen and shared by hundreds of thousands of people, she was as candid as President Trump: "Do you care about Black lives? The people that run Baltimore don't." In the video, Kim walks through the real streets of Baltimore. The buildings are boarded up. The weeds are growing through cracks in the sidewalk. The graffiti is as clear as day. This is a city that no person would feel safe in.

And why should they feel safe? Kim doesn't mince her words. "Baltimore is one of the top five most dangerous cities in America. The murder rate in Baltimore is ten times the US average. The Baltimore poverty rate is over 20 percent. Homicide, drug, and alcohol deaths are skyrocketing in our city." As Kim points out, this is the result of the Democratic Party controlling Baltimore for the past fifty-three years. The title of her video should be a bumper sticker on the back of every Black American's car: "Black Lives Don't Matter to Democrats."

One of the things that Kim and I share is a passion for people. We love to hit the streets to talk to the people who live, work, and raise their kids in our cities. When Kim interviewed Black residents in Baltimore, it was clear that they too were fed up with the Democrats' nonsense. "Do you want to defund the police?" she asks a Black woman. "No," she responds. A Black man adds, "absolutely not." Another Black man tells her, "I had three sons killed in Baltimore city. And I think if we defund the police office, it's going to be worser than that." The other Black man asks, "What are you going to defund the police for? How are you going to defend your city?"

These are commonsense questions. But in the world of Democratic politics, common sense is in short supply. The Baltimore City Council voted to cut around $22 million from the police department's budget. City Council President Brandon Scott, who has since become Mayor Scott, put it this way: "These cuts are again what I'm going to say are responsible cuts to the police department budget that show that this council and the folks moving forward . . . are serious about changing the way we reallocate our funds." For residents like Kim and the folks she spoke to, it was clear that Baltimore was moving backwards under Democratic leadership.

Quite literally, the majority of people in that city did not want to defund the police. According to a poll conducted by the *Baltimore Sun*, 70 percent of residents did not support defunding the police. The people of Baltimore were clear: They did not support the Democratic Party's plan to further erode law and order in their city. Armstrong Williams, a contributor to the *Sun* who is himself Black, was just as taken aback by that demand as his city's constituents: "Either they've lost their minds, even if they've auctioned their souls, you just don't, in leadership, put the interest of your blindness ahead of people and the consequence. Some of these politicians have security forces. They live in lavish gated neighborhoods. A lot of poor people just don't live this way. They have to fight every day for food, for gas, for resources, and then they have to fight for their lives and their wellbeing."

It wasn't just about the number of police, it was also about the quality of the police. Jason Johnson, Baltimore's former Police Deputy Commissioner, said that because of the "defund the police" movement, Baltimore and cities across the country were confronting a staffing crisis. "Police agencies across the country are lowering their standards because they're seeing real increases in retirements and resignations and many, many fewer applicants. As result, they're having to lower their standards in who they're hiring to become police officers. This creates a danger to police professionalism and public safety. This would be reducing or eliminating requirements for college or prior work experience, changing the standards for prior drug use or criminal convictions, eliminating physical agility testing, eliminating cognitive testing. Those are the objective standards that have been changed by many law enforcement agencies."

This was the political climate in which Donald Trump, never one to soften the truth, tweeted about the "disgusting, rat and rodent infested mess" in Baltimore. According to President Trump, the city was "filthy." It was "dangerous." That didn't sit well with the Democrats. Caught with their pants down in the mess they had created, they tried to downplay the lived realities captured by Kimberly Klacik. "We have rats all over the country," said Mayor Bernard C. Young. Kamala Harris, who was then running for the Democratic nomination for president, said "It's disgraceful the president has chosen to start his morning disparaging this great American city." Other Democrats tried to paint Trump as a racist because he had also criticized Representative Elijah Cummings. But guess what? The Black Americans in Baltimore agreed with President Trump! Baltimore, a once great American city, wasn't great anymore. It was a rat and rodent infested mess under Democratic leadership. And everyone knew it.

Back in Virginia, my eyes were fixed on Baltimore like the rest of the nation. This was Baltimore, the city in which General Motors had once thrived for decades, providing blue-collar jobs to build our middle class. This was the city where other businesses had once emerged, thrived, and lifted up my fellow Americans along the way. Around the time Trump drew the nation's attention to the plight of Baltimore's residents, Fox Baltimore was reporting from the ground. "In downtown Baltimore, yet another business has announced it is moving out of the once bustling central business district." Barnes & Noble, Dick's Last Resort, and the Holiday Inn Hotel had all moved on from downtown and the inner harbor. Among the reasons they offered: the city's rising crime.

As I have already mentioned, and as I will no doubt mention again, I grew up watching *Star Wars*. I was enticed by the *Lord of the Rings*. The Galactic Empire. Sauron. The desire to accumulate power, to mystify the truth, and to leave a trail of suffering in your wake—this isn't just the grist of fantasy fiction. All of these epic stories, there's a reason they have remained so popular for so long. They're all allegories for the very real evil that exists in our world. I watched as Kamala Harris attacked our president because he wanted to save a dying city. If she was commenting from the outside, I might have believed that she was simply ignorant of the lived realities on the streets in Baltimore and that she was simply toeing her party's line. But her campaign headquarters were in Baltimore! That's like someone living inside a volcano saying it isn't hot.

To be fair, I understand why President Trump got in a bit of a mess. Unlike his colleagues in D.C., he's not one to soften the truth. If your city is a rat and rodent infested mess, he's going to call it a rat and rodent infested mess. You might not like how he says things, but you can't disagree with the truth of what he says. He was right. Baltimore was a disaster. And people, the real people who lived in Baltimore, and who didn't just have their political headquarters in Baltimore, knew it. These people have seen the rats in the streets where children play. They've seen the bloody syringes on the sidewalk. They've seen the murders, the abductions, and the other forms of gang violence. Our great president, he didn't create this mess. The Democrats did. President Trump, he was just holding the mirror.

In the wake of President Trump's criticism, everybody on the

Right was talking about Baltimore. They were posting photographs and footage. They were criticizing the Democratic Party and the politicians who had destroyed this city. There wasn't any confusion about who was responsible for the decay on display. But virtually no one was taking action. I'll be honest, I was disappointed. Everyone was pointing their fingers at the problem, but why was nobody doing anything? Why was nobody taking the first steps to solve these problems? Baltimore was dying and it seemed like everyone was just watching.

At the time, I had never been to Baltimore. I was disturbed by the photographs of used condoms on the streets. I was angered by the images of the homeless veterans, the crumbling buildings, and the Godzilla-sized rats. And I was let down because there wasn't any movement to solve these problems that we all knew were not going to be solved by the Democrats who held power in that city. If anything, we all knew the Democrats were going to make these problems much, much worse. Enough was enough. President Trump had sounded the Great Horn of Gondor. And I had heard it. It was time to act. I wanted to make Baltimore Great Again.

That day, I posted on social media. It wasn't a revolutionary post. It certainly wasn't a romantic post. I'm not a superhero and I don't monologue like one. What I posted that afternoon, it was just a simple post. It was short, it was sweet, and it was to the point. "I'm going to Baltimore to pick up trash." I didn't think too much about this post in the moment. Quite frankly, I was reminded of the way I felt after President Obama was re-elected in 2012. There was a problem that needed to be solved. If nobody was going to solve it, I was going to solve it myself. What am I going to do to realize the change that I want to see in the world? That's the question I've always asked myself. That's my upbringing shining through. My grandfather was a man of action. My father is a man of action. I am a man of action.

Everyone wanted to talk about how terrible the Democrats are. They're right, the Democrats are terrible! But that's not real political engagement. It's clicktivism. Real activism—that's boots on the ground. That's callused hands. That's conversations with real people in the real world. That said, social media is a wonderful tool. This device in my pocket, it's a door opener. It has changed my life in more ways than I can count. And it changed my life that day I posted about Baltimore. That post, in which I said I was going to Baltimore, it exploded like a supernova. Across the country, the support poured in. "I'm coming with you!" "Just tell me where and when!" "We're not going to let you clean up Baltimore alone!" I realized that the problem wasn't that people didn't want to act. It was that they needed a leader to get the ball rolling.

For the first time in human history, people were excited to pick up trash. We turned something very unsexy, very boring, and frankly very gross, into something fun. People were pumped. It was like a Kid Rock concert was about to go down. With the America First movement ready to hop in their cars, and on trains, and on planes, I messaged Kim Klacik. Mind you, at the time I lived in Northern Virginia. I had no connection to Maryland. I had no connection to Baltimore.

On July 28, 2019, I wrote to Kim, "Mrs. Klacik, Thank you so much for helping get out the word about the trash cleanup. I am planning on Monday, August 5th. Any suggestions on location would be a huge help!"

Kim wrote back, "Absolutely! I will be back out there this week and will write down the worst corridors that are still doable. I am sure some of the areas will need to be cleaned up by those that can dispose of needles. Thank you so much! I'll be there."

Here's the thing that a lot of people don't understand. You can't just show up to a city with an army of people. You need a permit. So we hopped through the bureaucratic hoops to get one. Every day, I had a guy on the ground in Baltimore. And every day he walked into the permit office to check on the status of our request. "Sorry, we don't have your permit ready." "I'm sorry, it's still not ready." "I'm so sorry, I really am, but we don't have a permit for you." It was the Friday before the cleanup that was scheduled to take place on Monday, and we still didn't have a permit.

I love my beautiful Americans who work for the government. I really do. Many of them pursued these roles because they truly love our country. But government inertia is a real problem. I couldn't believe something as benign and altruistic as a trash cleanup was not immediately approved. It is as if the slow gears of the governmental bureaucracy are designed to protect the status quo. As we all waited for the permit to be approved, I was reminded of a quote from President Ronald Reagan. "You can't be for big government," he said, "and still be for the little guy."

At this point, I said screw it. With no permit in hand, I decided that we were going to do it anyway. The Baltimore cleanup was not going to be stopped by governmental sluggishness, and if I'm going to be more cynical, what seemed like governmental unwillingness. Let's be honest. The Democrats were in power. The image of a bunch of Republicans traveling from all over the country to come and pick up their trash could not have been a less appealing image. But guess what? There were real people in these neighborhoods who really needed our help. In the same way Donald Trump has broken all the rules of politics as usual, I wasn't going to let their local government stop our movement. So what if we didn't have a permit? We had Americans with big hearts and even bigger wills. We had a real movement. That Monday, we descended on the city. The Baltimore cleanup had begun.

I'll be real, I didn't know what was going to happen. As I drove from Virginia to Maryland, I thought I might be arrested. The law was clear. And it was equally clear that we were about to break it. It was just as clear that I was the one who was leading this massive exercise in the public refusal to obey the law. But along with the uncertainty, there was also a visceral feeling of patriotism. Civil disobedience is one of the greatest American traditions. And it has a long history that goes all the way back to the Boston Tea Party. "Must the citizen ever for a moment, or in the least degree, hand over his conscience to the legislator?" asked Henry David Thoreau in his 1849 essay, "Civil Disobedience." For Thoreau, and so many other men who have made America great, what is legal should never take precedence over what is right. "I think that we should be men first, and subjects afterward," concluded Thoreau. "The only obligation which I have a right to assume, is to do at any time what I think right. It is not desirable to cultivate a respect for the law, so much as for the right." If Baltimore was going to jail me for picking up trash, then so be it.

On my journey as a political activist, I've learned that in most cases it's better to ask for forgiveness than permission. That's the mindset I had when I told that woman on my staff back in Virginia that she could go visit her Navy SEAL husband down in Florida. Was she breaking the rules by going? Yes. Was I breaking the rules by encouraging her to go? Yes. Is it possible we could have got permission for her to make that trip? Yes, it's certainly possible. But it was also possible that our request would have been denied. As

I mentioned, my work in Virginia was part of my education as a grassroots activist. And it's that "better to ask for forgiveness than permission" mindset that I had when I made the decision that I was going to pick up trash in Baltimore—permit or not.

President Trump said it best when he quoted the great military leader Napolean Bonaparte, "He who saves his country does not violate any law."

Moreover, even the worst moments can go viral in ways that produce a net positive. As I drove into the city, I couldn't help but imagine the photographs and video footage of what might happen. We weren't masked Antifa activists pouring into the city to break business windows, to attack police officers, and to otherwise turn Baltimore, Maryland into Portland, Oregon. We were here to help. We weren't dressed in Republican gear or Trump shirts. We were Americans helping Americans. If we were going to be punished for helping our fellow Americans, I wanted all of America to see it. I imagined the front page of newspapers across the country: *Scott Presler and hundreds of ordinary Americans arrested and thrown in jail for picking up trash.*

That Monday in Baltimore, I went to Home Depot. I'm walking up and down the aisles, I'm filling my cart with extra strength trash bags, and plastic gloves, and protective masks. I knew that we weren't cleaning up Central Park. We weren't just going to be picking up stray soda cans and old pizza boxes left by teenagers. This was a city crippled by drug abuse, and there were real risks involved. Trash, especially trash that's been rotting for ages, can grow mold and bacteria. If you inhale that, you're in trouble. If your trash bag rips and you get poked with a rusty nail, you're getting a tetanus shot. If your fingertip gets cut by a used needle, you're going straight to the emergency room.

By the time everyone showed up, we were ready to clean up Charm City. We met at the corner of North Fulton Avenue and Westwood Avenue at 8 a.m. to set up a tent with all the supplies. Immediately, we were drawing attention from the local neighborhood and several residents asked what we were doing. The answer was easy: "We're here to help." Over the next twelve hours, more than two hundred volunteers from all over the country came to pick up trash on the most dangerous streets in America. One family flew in from Utah; others drove up from Florida; and other volunteers came from Ohio, Pennsylvania, and Virginia. It truly was an act of love. Even my mom and dad came for the entire event. While I am an Eagle Scout, and I know a thing or two about organizing events, I want to make it clear that I could not have done this without them. After my tweets on Twitter went viral, Mom and Dad were with me every step of the way. They came with me to Home Depot to pick up supplies, drove several hours from Virginia to Maryland, and helped take care of every volunteer.

Mind you, this was a Monday. This wasn't the weekend. These were people who took time off from work to be here. They took time off from work to pick up trash. I'm getting chills as I write this, just remembering the feeling that was in the air. When Obama was running for president, liberals loved to talk about hope and change. To me, it was always just talk. But this was the real thing. The American spirit had filled the once great city of Baltimore.

When I was promoting the cleanup on social media, I didn't even make it political. I said, "This is Americans helping other Americans." This is not red. This is not blue. This is not Republican. This is not Democrat. We're not making this political. This isn't about Trump. This is about America first. We're all Americans first. We see a problem. We come together to solve it. We all want to do the right thing. We all want to do the good thing—even if it's not the easy thing. This is what the American spirit is all about.

From 8 a.m. to 8 p.m., we picked up trash.

To be honest, most of the people who traveled to Baltimore to help me were white. Sure, we had people from different races, but for the most part this was a group of white Americans walking through the streets of a predominantly Black neighborhood. Naturally, the residents in the neighborhood were asking themselves and each other: What the heck is going on out there? A lot of these people came out of their houses. They were walking over to us. They were talking to us. They were like, "Wait, what? You flew here to pick up trash in our neighborhood?" and "You're taking a vacation day to be here?" and "You've never even been to Baltimore before?" I told them, "We heard President's Trump's call." There were problems in this city, and these people needed our help.

The response was so overwhelmingly positive. Across the board, the people in this neighborhood thanked us. Many of them actually asked for gloves, masks, and trash bags, too. They wanted to help us clean up their streets. The videos and photographs from that day are truly amazing. I'm six-foot-five inches tall. I'm in my thirties. I was born in Florida. I talk with an accent. I'm as white as a loaf of Wonder Bread. And my favorite thing ever, we had this eighty-one-year-old woman, Miss Louise, who stepped out of her house to stand with us. She's a Black woman. She's four-foot-eleven inches tall. She's just this tiny little thing. At one point, she invited us inside her home. There's a video of her and me walking together. It's my six-foot-five shadow towering over her four-foot-eleven silhouette. I'm still holding a trash bag. Her ceiling is so low I had to duck my head to get inside. It's like, gosh, these are the great American stories that I wish the mainstream media would tell. This is the American spirit of unity that doesn't get attention.

And it wasn't just Baltimore. When we started cleaning up other cities, it was the same outpouring of support. I met this woman, really just the sweetest little thing, when we were in Texas. She had the Arkansas twang in the way she talks. It's a great thing. She showed up with her little walker. She drove all the way from Arkansas to help us pick up trash in Dallas, Texas. (Yes, Miss Judy, I'm writing about you and I can't wait to give you a signed copy of this book.) She drove that far to pick up trash. She drove that far to pick up trash in the middle of the summer in one-hundred-degree weather in the great state of Texas, where the humidity is so thick you can cut it with a knife. You know what she told me? She said, "Scott, I'm doing this for you. I had to come here. I had to drive all this way just to meet you. I just respect you so much. And I love the work that you're doing." If that doesn't speak to the great American spirit in this country, then I don't know what does.

During another cleanup in Texas, I think it was in Austin, we saved a cat. We were just picking up trash and this sweet little baby was purring in the rubble. Someone got a box. They took off their sweatshirt and made a little bed for it. That cat went on to sleep in that person's bed before we got it into a home. It's these kinds of stories that show you it's more than just trash. It's our homeless veterans. It's our children playing in the streets. It's stray dogs and stray cats wandering through the wreckage of American cities looking for food and a place to keep them safe from the snow and the rain. Remember? I was a dog walker before I became a political activist. And it pains me to see these animals just lying in the wreckage of liberal cities. A lot of this stuff, you can't ever unsee it. And it's those images, burned into my brain, that inspire me to keep fighting to save our country.

The people in these cities, they see the work we're doing. They see Republicans like that little Arkansas woman with her walker, picking up trash. They see Republicans like the man who took off his sweatshirt and found a shoebox to save that poor cat. We're opening hearts and minds—and we're changing lives, too. It's not just a facade. It's not just on its face. It's not just skin deep. We're changing this country, one person, one voter at a time. That work, as the results of 2024 showed—77,302,580 votes to 75,017,613 votes—has paid off. And mark my words, if we stick with it, if we continue to put in the work, if we continue to show the rest of the country what the Republican Party is all about—putting Americans first—it's only going to continue to pay off in ever bigger and better ways. One day, one city, and one state at a time, we're Making America Great Again.

Here's one more story: When we were setting up our canopy in Baltimore, we saw a Black woman walking her dog. It was so small, it must have been a Chihuahua. She and this little morsel of a dog walked over to us. She's like, "What are you guys doing?" Again, we were a group of hundreds of white people in this predominantly Black neighborhood who had virtually appeared out of thin air on a Monday morning. If I was her, I would be asking questions too! I said, "We're doing a cleanup. We want to do something positive. We're here to help. You're welcome to join us." She was like, "Yeah, I'll come back later." And she did come back later. We picked up trash together. We laughed together. There's a great photograph of her hugging me.

This woman, she was Freddie Gray's aunt.

The liberal media would have flooded Baltimore had we been a group of left-wing environmental activists or Black Lives Matter activists. There would have been news crews, and anchors, and photographers all over the place. The liberal media loves to present the Left as the good guys, the ones who are saving the world from climate change, and racism, and poverty, and every other problem under the sun. I imagine they would have flocked around Freddie Gray's aunt, somehow trying to spin her presence into votes for the Democratic Party. This is what the liberal media does. It functions as the propaganda machine of the Democratic Party.

Can you imagine MSNBC giving the spotlight to a bunch of white MAGA supporters exchanging hugs and sharing laughs with the Black residents of a run-down neighborhood in Baltimore? Those kinds of stories aren't going to air because they don't fit the narrative. Their narrative is that everyone who voted for Trump is a racist. Their narrative is that Republicans don't care about people like Miss Louise and Freddie Gray's aunt. Perhaps above all else, the liberal media loves to sow the seeds of racial division. Can anyone imagine Rachel Maddow or Nicole Wallace celebrating the Baltimore Cleanup? That kind of story doesn't fit their narrative.

Democrats Destroy Cities

It also doesn't fit the interests of the Democratic Party. For decades, the Democrats have been pandering to minority communities. Instead of going into their cities and solving their day-to-day problems, the Democrats would rather produce utterly moronic videos touting their racial bona fides. Do you remember that 2020 video featuring presidential candidate Mayor Pete Buttigieg? It's real. But it looks like a *Saturday Night Live* sketch. In it, Mayor Pete is in an inner-city neighborhood drinking alcohol out of a brown paper bag with two Black guys. In the words of Black political scientist Wilfred Reilly: "Is Buttigeg drinking a 40 in the hood the apex modern example of political pandering? If not, what is?" Mayor Pete could have used that time to help us clean up the Black neighborhoods in Baltimore. But that's not part of the Democrats' playbook.

The Democrats would much rather monologue about their increasingly esoteric definitions of "white supremacy," and "white fragility," and "whiteness," and how supposedly racist Donald Trump is. After all, it was President Biden who denounced white supremacy as the "most dangerous terrorist threat" to the nation during his commencement address at the historically Black Howard University. Please tell that to the families of those who died on September 11, 2001. Please tell that to the police officers who are fearing for their lives because Antifa is waging terrorist attacks, including those in Seattle, Washington, who saw their precinct taken over. It was Senator Elizabeth Warren who said President Trump has "done everything he can to stir up racial conflict and hatred in this country." Aside from the pure emptiness of those kinds of claims, these politicians don't solve any of the problems in the Black community. They actually just stoke the virulent racial divisions and hatred they purport to be against.

In 2020, the number of Black homicide offenders was 310. The number of white homicide offenders was 56. The number of Black homicide victims was 472. The number of white homicide victims was 97. In 2019, the numbers were similar. The number of Black homicide offenders in Baltimore was 268. The number of white homicide offenders was 71. The number of Black homicide victims was 451. The number of white homicide victims was 88. Black residents make up 29.89 percent of Baltimore's population. These horrifying statistics, which every political leader in Baltimore should feel ashamed about, are not going to be corrected with more "unconscious bias" training seminars from Ibram X. Kendi and Robin DiAngelo. These problems confronting the city of Baltimore are not problems of "white supremacy."

Likewise, when we stepped foot in Baltimore at the end of 2019, "white supremacy" wasn't the reason there were bloody syringes, used diapers, and broken alcohol bottles on the sidewalks and in the streets where children play. "Whiteness" had nothing to do with any of these problems. To anyone who was willing to view the situation objectively, these were so clearly problems of failed Democratic leadership. Yet, that's not what President Biden, Senator Warren, Mayor Pete "40 in the hood" Buttigieg, and the Black Lives Matter movement will tell you. It most certainly is not what the liberal media establishment will tell you.

In his book *The ALL NEW Don't Think of an Elephant! Know Your Values and Frame the Debate*, George Lakoff, a cognitive linguist and advisor to the Democratic Party, is clear about the war over ideas, what he calls *framing*. "Framing is about thought, about understanding at the deepest levels, about circuity in your brain with strong synapses that last, about changing unconscious, automatic, effortless understanding—in other words, about changing common sense." For years, the liberal media establishment has perpetuated the frame that Republicans do not care about racial minorities. They have perpetuated the frame that Democrats are the "allies" of racial minorities. In some corners of public discourse, this is common sense. This frame is apparent in how they tell their stories. It is also apparent in their decision to not tell the stories that don't fit inside their frame.

This is why President Trump's tweet was so widely decried by the Democrats. According to their frame, Baltimore was a shining city on the hill, one that shined so bright because of decades of Democratic leadership. It was a city where Black Americans had stood behind their Democratic saviors. It was a city that proved that the Democrats were the only party for urban minority voters. In reality, it was a "rat and rodent infested mess." I remember seeing a group of children playing outside. There was a big fat dead rat in the middle of the strip of asphalt where they were playing. Its corpse was just eroding in the Baltimore sun. God forbid one of these children slipped and fell on it. This isn't a stray newspaper. This is a dead animal that can spread disease. I remember thinking to myself, how is that a way to live? Is this what America has become? I saw it with my own eyes. Perhaps, that's part of the problem. For some living in Baltimore, that's a normal occurrence.

To democrats in Orange County, California, however, they may not even fathom this reality. How can we do a better job of popping the hypocritical bubble that so many rose-colored-glasses-wearing voters live in and how do we do it in such a way that they don't immediately recoil from seeing the truth?

In Baltimore, I and the hundreds of people who joined me could not have been more excited to clean up the city that Democrats had trashed.

In Los Angeles, it was even worse. We needed hazmat suits. That is how disgusting L.A. has become. We needed hazmat suits like we were cleaning out Jeffrey Dahmer's apartment in Milwaukee. This wasn't a toxic waste dump. This is a place that our American brothers and sisters, sons and daughters, and mothers and fathers call home. Back in 2019, Trump was absolutely correct when he said, "California is a disgrace to our country. It's a shame. The world is looking at it. Look at Los Angeles with the tents and the horrible, horrible disgusting conditions."

This is a president who isn't afraid to call out baloney.

And the people who joined me when I headed to L.A. weren't afraid to put in the work to make the City of Angels great again.

In Los Angeles, even the homeless people joined us. They grabbed gloves and masks. They put on hazmat suits. One of these people, his name was Bear. And, I'll be honest, he looked like a bear. He was taller than me. And he was muscular, really muscular. In his prime, I imagine he could have been a lineman in the NFL. Bear, he slept on the streets at night. During the day, he worked in film and television. He said, "I work all the time, and I still can't afford to live here." The Democrats love to hector people about gentrification, but it's their party who has pushed people like Bear out of houses and apartments and into the streets. Los Angeles hasn't elected a Republican mayor since 2001.

By the way, remember how we picked up twelve tons of trash in twelve hours in Baltimore? We picked up fifty tons of trash from Van Nuys. And remember how we didn't have a permit to pick up trash in Baltimore? We didn't have one for Los Angeles either. We kept everything underground—not posting any locations or identifying videos until the morning of the cleanup. In fact, after we began picking up tens of tons of garbage, a police officer came by. I spoke with him and he told me that if he had known we were going to do this, he would have shut it down. Since we were already on site, he wasn't going to stop us.

What made me lose even more faith in government in general

is when I learned that the federal government was leasing the land to California. California wasn't going to clean up the trash because it's federal property. The federal government wasn't going to help because the property is in California's hands. Why did it take a long-haired, boot-wearing conservative to travel thousands of miles across the country to a state completely controlled by Democrats to show more love to our citizens and our land than they have for years? You may wonder what happens to these locations after we pack up and go home. I often do, too. Is it just a Band-Aid? Is it just a feel-good story? Are we making a difference? A few months after the L.A. cleanup, an NBC reporter followed up with me:

"Hey Scott! John from NBC in Los Angeles. City finally came and cleared out the encampment you cleaned up. That was Nov 19. Today the area is still empty. Not what we usually see. Wanted to share that with you. City is considering turning the vacant lot into a 'safe parking' area for people who live in their vehicles."

I responded, "Wow. Thank you for sharing this. Do we know what happened to the people who were living there?"

"Scattered. Thirty total. Five agreed to housing."

It's moments like this one that I think about "The Star Thrower." This is the story where a man criticized a young boy for throwing starfish into the sea that were going to die from a low tide. Then, the boy picked up another starfish, threw it into the water, and said, "I made a difference to that one."

For the five members of the homeless community that agreed to housing, we made a difference. To the hundreds of volunteers that dedicated their time to cleaning up their community, we made a difference. To every person that saw the news reports of concerned citizens coming together in an act of love—which has likely inspired other cleanups—we made a difference. One theme that you'll see again and again in this book is the power of one. We are distinctly in control of our own destinies. The question is: When you see a problem, will you wait for permission to act or will you be the solution and become your own hero? Above all, when the road is long and the destination is uncertain, will you persist?

About a quarter of the country's homeless population now lives in the once great state of California. The policies of Democrats and homelessness go together like peanut butter and jelly.

It's difficult to find one without the other.

Of course, Los Angeles wasn't my first rodeo.

One of the worst cities in the country, it's a place called Kensington, Pennsylvania. It's a neighborhood in Philadelphia. According to *Grid Magazine*, one-third of Philadelphia's homeless population resides in Kensington. It's bad, really bad. And you know what it has in common with L.A.? You know what it has in common with Baltimore? You know what it has in common with San Francisco? L.A. is Democrat. Baltimore is Democrat. San Francisco is Democrat. Philadelphia is Democrat. At this point, it's so obvious. When Democrats come to power, businesses leave. Americans lose their jobs and their health insurance. They get pushed into the streets, where open-air drug markets proliferate and the police have been defunded. When Democrats are in power, prisons empty and the homeless population rises faster than a Pacific Ocean wave. These cities where Democrats hold power, they quite literally crumble to the ground.

It's ordinary Americans—not Nancy Pelosi living on her California vineyard—who have to sleep in the rubble.

To be clear, many homeless people are drug addicts, alcoholics, and they do refuse to work. They end up in California where drugs have been decriminalized. In California, they are handing out drugs to addicts. I'm not exaggerating when I say that if you're a drug addict who wants to continue using drugs, there are few places in the world better than the state of California.

But there's another kind of homeless person. There's the homeless person who has paid his dues, and who has worked hard, and who has lived a moral life, and who—because of Democratic leadership—is still sleeping in the streets. In reality, many of our homeless are like Bear. They are altruistic, they are smart, and they are hardworking. But Democratic policies have created insurmountable challenges to a basic standard of living, much less a middle-class life.

Most disturbing, many of our homeless are veterans. According to the National Coalition for Homeless Veterans, "5.3% of the homeless adult population are veterans. 20% of the male homeless population are veterans. 68% reside in principal cities." As our US Department of Veterans Affairs puts it, "being homeless, or being at risk of homelessness, is one of the most difficult problems any Veteran can face." They're right. And the policies of Democratic city leaders are doing our veterans no favors.

These are the policies that put criminal illegal aliens—not American heroes—first.

Recently, the US Department of Housing and Urban Development released a report on the state of homelessness across the nation. In it, they conclude: "Migration had a particularly notable impact on family homelessness, which rose 39% from 2023-2024. In the 13 communities that reported being affected by migration, family homelessness more than doubled. Whereas in the remaining 373 communities, the rise in families experiencing homelessness was less than 8%."

In Los Angeles, I couldn't help but ask the same question I had asked a young progressive woman in San Francisco in that video on the streets that went viral: Why do Democrats care more about criminal illegal aliens than American citizens like Bear? Why would they rather usher in caravans of criminal illegal aliens than affordable housing for the veterans who risked life and limb to protect our freedoms?

None of this is open to debate. You can't flood America's labor market with cheap, illegal labor and expect there not to be consequences for the American citizens who live here.

I know Representative Pelosi isn't worried about losing her job to a criminal illegal alien. I know she isn't worried about getting catapulted into poverty. But the ordinary Americans—including many great Californians who live in her own state—*are* worried. And their worries are absolutely justified. The data doesn't lie. It tells a crystal-clear story about the failure of Democratic leaders.

I'll ask it again: Why do Democrats care more about criminal illegal aliens than American citizens like Bear?

Why do they care more about protecting bad hombres than the men and women who have fought courageously to protect our freedoms?

From Los Angeles to Kenosha and Philadelphia, why are Democrats intent on destroying city after city after city?

If you look at the data, I'm not the only one asking that question. In 2024, ten out of California's fifty-eight counties flipped from blue to red. They voted for President Trump. They voted for the only candidate who was willing and capable of securing our nation's border and deporting every last criminal illegal alien. Under the last administration, these criminal aliens knew that our president was soft on immigration. They knew that the United States was theirs for the taking. This isn't my opinion. This is a fact. Remember 2021? That was President Biden's first year in office. "The U.S. Border Patrol reported more than 1.6 million encounters with migrants along the U.S.-Mexico border in the 2021 fiscal year, more than quadruple the number of the prior fiscal year and the highest annual total on record," writes the Pew Research Center. In 2020, the last year President Trump was in office, that number was just over four hundred thousand. The difference between a Democratic president and a Republican president is palpable.

It's most palpable for people like Bear. While Governor Gavin Newsom doesn't have to worry about a criminal illegal alien pushing him out of his home—a $9.1 million, six-bedroom, six-bathroom mansion with a swimming pool and an inset spa—everyday Americans like Bear do. Criminal illegal aliens steal affordable housing. They steal governments benefits. They steal jobs. The Democrats love criminal illegal aliens because they're the ones who clean their mansions and take care of their kids for low wages. Just look at Dianne Feinstein, the Democrat who served as a United States senator from California from 1992 until her death in 2023. Her Guatemalan maid was an illegal.

Like President Trump, I am pro worker. I am pro union. I am pro ICE. They just arrested seventeen illegal aliens in Bethlehem, Pennsylvania. These aliens were working—illegally—on a property construction site. That's seventeen jobs that could have gone to union workers. That's seventeen jobs that could have provided a meaningful wage and health insurance to seventeen Americans who were born here. If the Democrats wanted to appeal to working-class people, who are now definitively voting for Republicans in our elections, they would start by relinquishing their support for cheap, illegal labor. Americans will never have livable wages as long as criminal illegal aliens are willing to work under the table for slave wages. For all their prattle about the legacy of slavery in this country, it's the Democrats who keep it alive. Certainly, Senator Feinstein could have afforded to pay a native-born American worker in a union to wash her windows and sweep her kitchen floors.

The Democrats do not care about working-class Americans.

More significantly, the Democrats love criminal illegal aliens because criminal illegal aliens love to vote for Democrats. As the 2020 election showed, illegals steal votes just like they steal housing, benefits, and jobs. According to *National Review*, "the net effect of increases in both legal and illegal immigration in the 2020 Census shifted 17 House seats and 17 Electoral College votes, resulting in a net gain of 14 seats in Blue States—ten seats shifting from red states and four from battleground states. That Democratic net gain is greater than the respective electoral votes of *all but ten states*." As they conclude, "of the 24 districts where one in five adults is not an American citizen, 20 were won by a Democrat in 2022. In contrast, the Democrats won in just five of the 54 districts where 98 percent of adults are citizens." In this landscape, the Democrats don't need to worry about winning over Americans like Bear. They just need to replace Americans like Bear. This makes the 2028 presidential election all the more important. Whoever controls the White House controls redistricting going into the 2030 Census. Do you think democrats are just going to lie down and relinquish power so easily? No, the next presidential election is going to be one for the history books. From red refugees fleeing blue states into Idaho, Florida, and Texas, Republicans are going to pick up seats. You'll probably see a net gain of ten electoral points from interstate migration alone. The census could very well decide who wins the presidency for the next decade.

If you think sanctuary cities are about protecting political refugees and other vulnerable people from other countries, you're not paying attention. The push to turn every American city into a sanctuary city is about what is has always been about: *votes*.

The ideal election for a Democratic politician is one in which as many criminal illegal aliens as possible are sneaking into the polls.

That is not my opinion. That is what the data says.

And every Democratic Party strategist knows it.

One of the things that frustrates me most about Democrats is that they will acknowledge problems like urban homelessness, and then they will promote policies that make these problems significantly worse in their cities. At the time I am writing this book, Zohran Kwame Mamdani has just been elected Mayor of New York City. Somehow this son of a Columbia University professor has branded himself as a man of the people, a socialist who ran on a platform to uplift poor and working-class New Yorkers. As part of his wildly impractical agenda, Mamdani wants to raise the minimum wage to $30 an hour by 2030. Do you know what that would do to NYC? Businesses would be fleeing that city faster than they fled it during the COVID lockdown. After Mamdani won the Democratic primary, real estate professionals in Florida reported a surge in interest from New York City–based investors. When businesses leave, it's not Columbia University professors who lose their jobs. It's poor and working-class people who lose their jobs. These Americans, they end up in the streets.

It's not just the minimum wage. It's Mamdani's other policies. How do you have a rent freeze in New York City? Jay Batra, a real estate entrepreneur and the principal of Batra Real Estate, a full-service real estate brokerage in New York City and Miami, told *Newsweek*: "Our clients who own buildings across NYC are deeply concerned about the rent freeze tied to Mayor Mamdani's agenda. Landlords are facing mounting pressure—with high taxes and operating costs, it's becoming unsustainable to hold properties without the ability to adjust rents. Many are now evaluating out-of-state investments as a safer, more profitable alternative." Florida Council of 100, a nonprofit, nonpartisan organization of Florida business leaders who advise the state's governor, wrote a letter to NYC business leaders. "Today, New York's future feels increasingly uncertain—an unacceptable risk for business leaders responsible for their businesses and the families that rely upon them," they wrote, "Florida offers a better path." In other words, the better path for businesses, and everyday people who depend on them for employment, is the path away from cities controlled by Democrats.

When businesses flee cities controlled by the Democratic Party, do you think that raises wages? Do you think that gets more homeless people off the streets and into good paying jobs with health insurance and other benefits? Of course it doesn't. You can't end poverty without jobs! And you can't have jobs without the capitalists who create them. I know socialists like Mamdani and the folks at *Jacobin* magazine hate the word "capitalist." And I know they are part of a socialist tradition that is willing to use violence against capitalists. Karl Marx reportedly wrote, "the last capitalist we hang shall be the one who sold us the rope." But revolutionary violence is not how you solve problems in the real world. You solve problems by supporting the people who create jobs—not by killing them. The fact that we now have to explain this to the rising socialist movement across the country, which is supporting politicians like Mamdani, is a sign of just how insane the state of the union has become.

In September of 2025, Gallup reported where we are heading as a country. As Ryan King summarized the results of the poll: "Americans' approval of capitalism has plunged to a record low, while their support for socialism has ticked up slightly in recent years, a new Gallup poll shows. Only 54% of US adults surveyed said they have a positive image of capitalism, the lowest level Gallup has recorded since it began asking the question 15 years ago. That's down sharply from 60% support in 2021." As King notes, the drive is coming from Democrats. "Democrats' view of capitalism dropped from 50% positive in 2021 to 42%. That's the first time the group's approval amount dipped below 50%. . . . The boost for socialism comes amid the rise of lefty Democratic socialists such as Sen. Bernie Sanders (I-Vt.), Rep. Alexandria Ocasio-Cortez (D-NY), and New York City Democratic mayoral hopeful Zohran Mamdani."

Meanwhile, "Republicans' love of capitalism increased from 72% in 2021 to 74%."

Another strategy in the Left's war on capitalists, which is now destroying cities like Los Angeles and Baltimore just like it destroyed cities like Detroit and Flint, Michigan, is their murder by taxation. If you tax the heck out of businesses, you're going to kill them. This is especially true for small businesses, the backbone of the American dream. These business owners, who are smart, are understandably going to flee your city like the plague. Why would they stay in a city where their profits are going to be robbed by government bureaucrats? Why would they stay in a city where they're not going to be able to make ends meet? Ironically, while the socialist Left loves to talk about the working class, who is now decisively voting Republican, it is their tax policies that prevent business owners from raising their employees' salaries and wages. There's only so much to go around, and there's going to be even less to go around when the left-wing government is sticking its hands in your wallet.

Moreover, if you tax the heck out of ordinary people, they're not going to be able to stay in their homes. Why should a senior citizen on a fixed income who is sixty-five years old have to pay property taxes? Why should they have to pay increasingly expensive property taxes when they're already paying for rising food, gas, electricity, water, and internet costs?

Heck, I'm going to write it right here and now: *abolish property taxes*.

If Republican legislatures begin abolishing property taxes across the country, it will be one of the largest transfers of generational wealth in American history. Two of the core beliefs of the Republican Party are that education and property ownership are the best ways to combat poverty. To continue with property taxes is to continue under the charade of government slavery. How is that an approach to keeping our nation's elders out of poverty? According to the Kaiser Family Foundation, "About 6 to 8 million adults ages 65 and older were living in poverty in 2022, depending on the measure used to assess poverty. Under the official poverty measure, one in 10 (10.2%), or 5.9 million adults ages 65 and older, had incomes below the official poverty threshold of $14,040 in 2022." As they explain, "The poverty rate was higher based on the Supplemental Poverty Measure, 14.2% or 8.2

million older adults, primarily because the Supplemental Poverty Measure takes into account out-of-pocket medical expenses that are not incorporated in the official poverty measure."

It's especially bad in locations controlled by Democrats. In 2015, the mayor of Washington D.C., was a Democrat. In 2011, the mayor was a Democrat. In 2007, the mayor was—you guessed it—a Democrat. Washington has never had a Republican mayor. Since the first mayor was elected in 1975, our capital city has been controlled by the Democratic Party. D.C. is a microcosm of Democratic leadership, and it's one that reveals a lot about the damage this party does to the Americans who live in our cities. In D.C., 23 percent of people age sixty-five and older have incomes below the poverty threshold. As the Poor People's Campaign notes, "Washington, D.C. is home to 148,000 poor and low-income eligible voters who make up 21.5% of the electorate." When you think about what the Democrats have done to D.C., you should think about it as a model for what they will do to every city in the United States of America.

Property taxes, which Democrats always want to increase, are a big part of the story of our national poverty and homelessness crisis. I've met people in Chicago who have been unable to afford to stay in their homes, homes that they have already paid off, because of property taxes. Even worse, I've met Chicago residents who are now renting homes they used to own. That is the opposite of what Republicans are trying to accomplish. But in the case of Democrats, it looks like it is by design.

In 2025, the Illinois Policy Institute reported that the "Typical property tax bill increased 78% on a Cook County residence since 2007. Median property values only rose 7.3%. That leaves residents paying $2,558 more a year in property taxes while their biggest investment fails to keep up with inflation." They published this report after Mayor Brandon Johnson, a Democrat, proposed a $300 million property tax *increase*. I'm sorry, but that is absolutely preposterous. It's little more than a formula for turning homeowners into homeless.

After being catapulted into homelessness by the Democrats, the Democrats then use the homeless as their mascots. They become the mascots for policies—higher taxes, lax drug laws, etc.—that will catapult even more Americans into homelessness. "For four semesters a quarter-century ago," reflects Marvin Olasky, "I taught nearly two thousand University of Texas at Austin freshmen and sophomores how to think critically about both liberals and conservatives—but I did show my moderate conservatism by using as a primary textbook free market economist Thomas Sowell's *The Vision of the Anointed*." As Olasky explains, "Maybe I could get away with that because Sowell, now 94, is not only brilliant but Black. Several students did complain, particularly about a section Sowell titled 'Mascots of the Anointed.' The 'anointed,' Sowell showed, were those in academia and media who thought they knew how to reconstruct American society, and adopted particular groups as 'mascots, often without much regard for what that does to other groups or to the integrity of the system as a whole.'"

If you want to raise taxes on businesses (driving business owners out of the city), talk about the homeless.

If you want to raise the minimum wage (driving business owners out of the city), talk about the homeless.

If you want to raise property taxes (driving homeowners into poverty and eventually out of the city), talk about the homeless.

How do you help the homeless? In the eyes of the Democrats, you promote policies that lead to more homelessness. How do you clean up the tents in Los Angeles? You promote policies that lead to even more tents in Los Angeles. How do you clean up the bloody syringes, empty pill bottles, and Ziploc bags on the streets of Baltimore? You pass policies that increase the amount of bloody syringes, empty pill bottles, and Ziploc bags on the streets of Baltimore.

How do you save native-born workers in Texas, Arizona, and New Mexico? You flood the market with cheap undocumented labor by defunding border patrol and ICE. How do you rebuild the African American community? You find a pair of Black men and drink alcohol out of a paper bag with them like Mayor Pete Buttigieg. From the perspective of the Democratic Party, this is how you build an America that works for everyone.

This is the upside-down, topsy-turvy, *Alice in Wonderland* world of the Democratic National Committee, our universities, and the liberal media establishment who work in cahoots to further harm the cities and the people they purport to save. This is the world that President Donald Trump and the Make America Great Again movement are working to change. This is the world that our America First movement *will* change.

Cleaning Up After the Left

In addition to the Democratic National Committee, our universities, and the liberal media establishment, there's another force that is destroying our cities and our country. That force is the activist Left. I'm not talking about The Squad. I'm talking about the progressives who burned down Kenosha, Wisconsin.

During the Summer of Love—an Orwellian misnomer if I have ever heard one—when the riots over George Floyd's death were tearing this country apart, the Left traveled to this Midwest city. It's estimated that about fifty or more businesses were targeted by the left-wing rioters. One of those businesses, The Good Taste Ice Cream Shoppe, was burned to the ground.

Miguel Anguiano Hernandez had opened the shoppe sixteen years earlier. It was a family business, with about 10 of the children in his family helping out. In sixteen years, no one had even broken a window. By the time the Left left, the Good Taste Ice Cream Shoppe was engulfed in flames.

"Everything burned to the ground," Hernandez's daughter told *The Daily Signal*. "Expensive machines, compressors. I mean, things that you cannot even think they're going to burn because it's metal. . . . It's just garbage." This is what the Left does. Whether it's the politicians in office or the Black Lives Matter activists in the streets, they turn beautiful cities into ashes.

We went to Kenosha right after that happened.

We were there cleaning up the debris.

We were there cleaning up after the Left.

It was horrible.

Fox Business reported that the damage topped $50 million. There was graffiti everywhere. Picking up burned pieces of buildings and seeing how people, including many people of color, had lost everything, I couldn't help but feel anger. What happened to George Floyd was atrocious. It was disgusting. It was rightfully criticized by those on the Left and the Right. In the words of Secretary of State Marco Rubio, "the murder of Mr. Floyd at the hands of law enforcement officers was an outrageous crime that has shocked this nation." I pray for the family members of George Floyd and anyone who has seen a loved one killed.

But how was turning Good Taste Ice Cream Shoppe—an immigrant of color's dream—into a pile of ashes supposed to make this loss better? How is arson a rational response to this tragedy? How does it prevent the use of excessive force by police officers? How was looting innocent people's stores and homes supposed to make our country a safer place? Why are the people who talk ad nauseum about "social justice" some of the people who contribute the most to injustice?

When you zoom out, it quickly becomes apparent that many people on the Left aren't good people. They're bad people who try to justify their bad actions by using good words: justice, equality, and so on.

Moreover, if the cops are so corrupt, and violent, and outright evil, then why is the Left trying to take away all our guns? If the people are stripped of their constitutional right to protect themselves, we're going to see a lot more businesses like the Good Taste Ice Cream Shoppe burn to the ground. As we all know, the bad people in our society will always find guns, even if they're outlawed. That leaves good people like the Santiago family totally unequipped to protect themselves.

When you look at the Left, it's clear that many of these people just love violence, and disorder, and mayhem. They, quite literally, are proud to call themselves anarchists. And Marxists. And revolutionaries. They will lecture you about Emma Goldman, and Noam Chomsky, and Karl Marx until the sun sets and the roosters crow in the morning. These people, they have no off switch. They're like the Energizer Bunny. They just keep going, and going, and going. But unlike the Energizer Bunny, they're wielding Molotov cocktails and sniper rifles. And they're going to keep going, and going, and going until American society as we know it is burned to the ground. I often find myself wondering if Democrats care more about destroying America than Republican voters care about saving her. While it often feels like pulling teeth to get conservatives engaged in elections, Democrats are like a dentist eager for extraction. They've got their pliers ready at a moment's notice.

That is what they mean when they talk about "dismantling structures" and "overthrowing systems" in their activist circles, academic journals, and trade publications. What systems and structures? In activist and scholar bell hooks's words, the "imperialist white supremacist capitalist patriarchy." hooks, who spelled her name with all lowercase letters as some kind discursive act of rebellion, is one of the most widely taught thinkers in humanities and social science departments on college campuses. The burned trash you see on the streets of Kenosha is really the physical embodiment of the intellectual trash that the Left has been feeding Americans for decades.

These are people who watch *Batman: The Dark Knight* and think the Joker is the hero of that film. "When I say that one little old mayor will die, well then everyone loses their minds. Introduce a little anarchy, upset the established order, and everything becomes chaos. I'm an agent of chaos. And you know the thing about chaos? It's fair," says the Joker. When Antifa took over Kenosha, and Portland, and Seattle, this was the world on fire envisioned by the Joker—and by anarchist movements from the past to the present. As Alfred tells Batman, "Some men aren't looking for anything logical . . . they can't be bought, bullied, reasoned, or negotiated with. Some men just want to watch the world burn."

Isn't that the flippant attitude toward human life that killed Charlie Kirk?

The man who killed Charlie wasn't going to be bought,

bullied, reasoned, or negotiated with. He was on the Utah Valley University campus to kill. The Left that rejoiced in Charlie Kirk's death couldn't understand why normal people were so upset. From the Left's perspective, Charlie was a threat. And threats need to be neutralized. "When I say that one little old conservative activist will die, everyone loses their minds" is basically what the Left was saying.

After his death, the far Left was truly unapologetic. "Charlie Kirk's Legacy Deserves No Mourning" was the headline at *The Nation*, a radical leftist publication that describes itself as the "principled" voice that "speaks truth to power to build a more just society." For its part, the socialist magazine *Jacobin* tried to whitewash history. "Political Violence Is Abhorrent. Charlie Kirk Didn't Think So." It was Kirk, they argued, who "fanned the flames of political violence."

But it was Kirk who was murdered!

It was Kirk who was teaching college students across the country to win through debate and reason—*not* violence.

In reality, it's the Left who fans the flames of violence. This is supported by the data. According to a recent YouGov poll, "Most Americans across the political spectrum say political violence is never justified, but younger and more liberal Americans are more likely to disagree." Indeed, 25 percent of Americans who identify as very liberal say "Yes, violence can sometimes be justified" in response to the question "Do you think it is ever justified for citizens to resort to violence in order to achieve political goals?" Among eighteen- to forty-four-year-old liberals, that number jumps to 26 percent. By contrast, just 3 percent of Americans who identify as "very conservative" agree. That's a whopping difference in attitudes toward political violence.

"The data is clear, people on the left are much likelier to defend and celebrate political violence," lamented Vice President JD Vance after the assassination of Charlie Kirk.

In all honesty, I don't need data to tell me that liberals are more likely to justify violence. We saw it. We saw it swiftly and immediately after Charlie's assassination. I didn't know what to do. I was so full of rage, anger, sadness, frustration, and a sense of powerlessness. I watched as thousands of people from across the country and beyond took to social media to celebrate murder.

"This may not be the obituary. We were all hoping to wake up to, but this is a close second for me," said Kelly Brock-Sanchez, a former elementary school teacher in Florida.

"A real pos!! Live by the sword die by the sword. F*** Charlie Kirk! The world is a better place without him," said Mark Sivek, a former board of directors' member of Las Vegas Realtors.

"No thoughts. No prayers. I hope the gun is ok," said Charlie Tousseull, a former Pima County librarian.

If the liberals are this cavalier in their attitude toward political violence, how do you think they feel about the destruction of property?

Pierre-Joseph Proudhon, considered by many to be the father of anarchism, proclaimed that "Property is Theft!" Today, many people on the Left share his attitude. As the socialist rock band Rage Against the Machine proclaims in their hit "War Within a Breath": "War within a breath/It's land or death/Their existence is a crime/Their seat their robe their tie/Their land deeds. . . . They're tha crime."

There's a reason our beautiful cities have seen so much destruction and chaos, and the reason is the Left.

The small handful of progressive journalists who are willing to ask commonsense moral questions—such as, how is it a form of social justice to burn innocent peoples' businesses to the ground?—get attacked by their colleagues and pushed out of liberal newsrooms. During the Summer of Love, Lee Fang, then a journalist at *The Intercept*, posted an interview with a Black man. In the video, the man says, "When people look at me, I'm Black. So when I, as a Black person, look at the Black Lives Matter movement, I have questions. Like, I always question, 'Why does a Black life matter only when a white man takes it?'" He goes on, "Where I grew up at in East Oakland, there's been a lot of Black people who [are] killed by other Black people, or Black people who will kill brown people, or vice versa. If a white man takes my life, it's going to be national news and stuff like that. If a Black man takes my life tonight, it might not even be spoken of." For simply talking to this Black man, thousands of people, including Lee's own colleagues at *The Intercept*, branded him a racist.

That's the progressive playbook in action.

You think vandalism is bad? You're a racist. You think arson is bad? You're a racist. You think assassination is bad? You're a racist.

Interestingly, progressives will even call Black people, like the man who Fang interviewed, racist. "He has internalized racism." "He has unconscious racial bias against his own people." "He is just a house negro." "He is just an Uncle Tom." "He is an Oreo, Black on the outside and white on the inside." It is not an overstatement to say that the most vicious attacks on ordinary Black people—the ones who aren't staff writers at the *New York Times* and professors at Harvard University—have come from the Left.

Racist is the all-encompassing magic word that can be used

to discredit people as different as Republican politicians and progressive journalists who momentarily fail to toe the line.

And it is a very, very effective accusation—even when it has as much truth in it as the idea that President Trump is colluding with Russia, that there's nothing to see on Hunter Biden's laptop, that COVID didn't come out of a Wuhan lab, and so on. If the Left is willing to suppress the truth about major issues like the global pandemic, then certainly they'll suppress an article by Lee Fang. The Left can only win when the truth is hard to find.

Like the Democratic Party's influence in Los Angeles, Chicago, and other cities, the trash in Baltimore had been there for decades. At one point, I found a 2008 newspaper in the debris. It was yellow. But it was so preserved because it had been under so much trash for more than a decade. The newspaper was celebrating President Obama's inauguration. The American people had been sold on the idea that Obama would bring positive change to the country, especially for Black Americans. Here I was looking at a relic of that unfulfilled promise. I still have that newspaper in my home. I plan to get it framed.

By the end of the day, we had picked up twelve tons of trash—twelve tons of trash in twelve hours. It was remarkable what we accomplished that day. It was also disheartening. We didn't have to walk through every neighborhood in Baltimore to pick up that much trash. We didn't have to walk miles to clear ton, after ton, after ton. We didn't even have to walk one mile. We cleaned up one neighborhood. The city was full of neighborhoods like this. By all means, I was so proud of what we had accomplished. It really was remarkable. But we had only cleared one mountain of trash from one neighborhood. There were mountains all over the city. As the day turned into night, I realized just how much damage the Democratic Party had done to Baltimore.

Like I said, I'm not a flash in the pan. I promised the people of Baltimore that we would be back. We came back every month for five months. Each time we visited that same neighborhood. Each time we were back in Baltimore we visited Miss Louise. We planted flowers in her garden. We celebrated her birthday with her. This wasn't a media blitz. And it wasn't even about politics. My team and I, we all cared about Baltimore. We all cared about residents like Miss Louise.

After Baltimore, I went on a cleanup tour across the country. At this point, I've led cleanups in Atlanta, Austin, Baltimore, Chicago, Denver, Duquesne, Detroit, Houston, Kenosha, Los Angeles, Miami, Milwaukee, Nashville, Portland, Pittsburgh, San Francisco, and Salem. I have been everywhere across this country. I have picked up, I don't know, hundreds of tons of trash. Needles. Bloody clothing. Human excrement. I mean, gosh, when we went to San Fransicko, it was absolutely sickening what we saw. Tent cities. Homeless people defecating in the streets. We were even protested for picking up trash. Yes, read that again. We were protested by Antifa for daring to pick up trash. They screamed—"go home, bigots!"—as volunteers made their city a cleaner place to live. It felt like we were in a third world country. With the sheer amount of criminal illegal aliens the Democrats have let into that city, it might as well be.

It was the same thing in Los Angeles. In about six hours, we picked up fifty tons of trash. You read that right: fifty tons of trash. It was a terrifying amount of trash, truly terrifying. But it wasn't just the amount. It was what was in the streets. There were dead animals. There were diapers filled with excrement. There were bloody clumps of hair. I actually found a shank. I wanted to keep it as a reminder of what the Democrats had done to L.A., but I had to fly home. In the City of Angels, we actually wore hazmat suits, masks, and goggles, like a nuclear bomb had hit and we were trying to avoid radiation. The videos are insane.

One study of the homeless population revealed just how bad this problem is not just for the homeless themselves, but for public health. "Overall, 95 % of survey respondents reported defecating outdoors; 36 % practiced outdoor defecation between 4 and 7 days/week and 27% practiced outdoor defecation <1 day/week. Of those that did practice outdoor defecation, 75% contained their feces in a bucket or bag." Imagine being a twelve-year-old girl walking to school, and you have to walk by an adult man defecating on the sidewalk. Imagine being an elderly person who has to step over human feces in front of their apartment complex. Imagine being a mother of two who has to hose urine off the front steps of their house. You don't have to imagine any of this. You just have to spend the weekend in Los Angeles.

Every city has homeless people. But what is so insane about L.A. was the sheer amount of homeless people living in this trash bin of a city. There's bubonic plague in L.A. There's typhus, which causes typhoid fever. According to the County of Los Angeles Public Health authorities, flea-born typhus has increased in L.A. county since 2010. In 2024, they set a record for new cases documented. There were close to two hundred cases. People with typhus have fevers, headaches, and rashes. They'll have nausea, and they'll vomit. For the first time since 1993, flea-borne typhus deaths are being reported. Los Angeles is a scary place. The people of this once great city deserve better than what the Democrats have given them.

Just think about this: A missionary had to have his foot amputated because it got infected when he was delivering food to a homeless encampment in L.A.—an American city, not a village in rural Africa. This encampment, it's on government property. But the government said, we don't have to clean it because we lease this property to the state of California. And the state of California said, we don't have to clean it because it's government property. So this is how the homeless live.

In September of 2025, journalists reported that a homeless "city" had emerged in Koreatown. From aerial photographs, it looks like a shanty town. Reportedly, people are running wires and stealing electricity from streetlights that they have pried open. The month before, a homeless man went viral for building a makeshift house in the trees. The man, who steals water from a nearby fire hydrant, said he sleeps in the trees to protect himself from getting mugged. You can't make this stuff up. "The reason why people are sleeping here is because you leaders are sleeping on not taking initiative and action to clean this place up," one neighborhood resident admitted in an interview about the homeless "city" that had sprawled up in Koreatown. Another neighborhood resident, a business owner, said "they stole two of my gate openers worth $8,000 each."

Democratic politicians still pretend to act confused when business leaders leave their cities.

If you want New York City to become the next Los Angeles, vote for Zohran Kwame Mamdani, your friendly neighborhood socialist.

When people think about Los Angeles, they think about places like Rodeo Drive, where palm trees and luxury stores decorate the streets. These are the places depicted in the movies. But this isn't a movie. And it isn't the Hollywood Hills, where liberal actors and actresses hold fundraising parties for the Democratic Party. This is the real L.A. The California of the 1960s and 1970s, which flourished under the leadership of Governor Ronald Reagan, really is a quaint memory of the past. California hasn't voted for a Republican president since 1988. Today, the City of Angels looks like the city of trash in *Wall-E*.

This isn't a shot at the people of L.A. Those beautiful Angelenos helped us clean up their city. And they too were frustrated with the bureaucratic malaise. After waiting for the permit that never arrived in Baltimore, we didn't even bother requesting one in California. In all seriousness, do you think they would have given it to us? Within thirty minutes of arriving, a police officer showed up. He said, "I shouldn't be telling you this, but if we had known you were going to do this, we would have stopped you. But since you're already here, we're not going to stop you." Of course he wanted to stop us. Did you think the LAPD was going to let their governor and mayor look this bad? Fortunately, there were hundreds of us. And we all had phones. They were smart enough to let us stay to avoid the viral media disaster that would have no doubt occurred had they tried to kick us out.

In the end, even though we weren't arrested, this was still terrible press for Governor Gavin Newsom—Governor Newscum, as President Trump calls him—and Mayor Eric Garcetti. This was their city. They were supposed to keep their streets clean and safe. They were supposed to take care of their people. That is what they were elected to do. That is their job! A bunch of Trump supporters had just removed fifty tons of trash—what artificial intelligence estimates is one football field full of trash more than two inches deep—from their city in just six hours. By the time we left, the obvious question was spreading like wildfire across social media and around the world: Why hadn't these Democratic politicians cleaned up their own city? If they were the party that cared about poor people, why did the part of California below their Hollywood Hills look like a toxic waste dump?

While we were cleaning, these Democrats were selling their own people short. The *New York Post* reported that Jennifer Siebel Newsom's nonprofit, Representation Project, "pays her a hefty $150,000—while raking in donations from companies that have an interest in winning the favor of her husband, California Gov. Gavin Newsom. AT&T, which has spent upward of $2 million to lobby the state on landline phone rules so far this year, forked over up to $25,000 for Representation Project's 'Flip the Script' gala." The people I met in Los Angeles, they're not going to fancy galas. And they don't have thousands of dollars to curry the favor of the "First Partner" of California—"First Lady" is, apparently, sexist—and her morally bankrupt husband.

When you look at the contrast between how the Newsoms live, and how the rest of their state lives, it is hard not to feel disenchanted. When you consider the sheer amount of trash still on the streets in their state, it is hard not to feel hopeless. We actually had an NBC reporter cover our volunteer work in the Van Nuys neighborhood of Los Angeles. He texted me three months after the cleanup. He said, "Scott, you're not making a difference." He said, "Those places that you clean, they're just going to become trash again. You're wasting your time. Why are you helping? It's not going to make a difference." But get this: Three months after he returned to the location, it was still clean. It's clean to this day.

Why? Because when people join hands to do something positive for their community, the effects are long lasting. Those are the stories that the media, especially in Democratic strongholds like Los Angeles, don't want to tell. Indeed, there's hardly anything more unappealing to liberal journalists and their liberal audiences than a story about Trump supporters doing something positive in their communities.

But guess what?

Those are the stories that make America great.

Our cleanups influenced other cities. Darius Mayfield, who ended up running for Congress in New Jersey, he started doing trash cleanups in blue cities like Newark and Camden. This inspired Philadelphia. Philadelphia, that's a city that has been wrecked by the Democrats. According to recent data, there are thousands of homeless people in that city. As Homelessness No More explains, "African Americans make up nearly 68% of the homeless population, despite accounting for about 40% of the city's overall population." The last eleven mayors, including current mayor Cherelle Park, have been Democrats. Aren't Democrats supposed to be the party for Black lives?

Even to this day, people will come up to me and say things like, "Scott, it doesn't sound like a lot, but in my neighborhood, when I bring my daughter over to the park to go play, I bring a trash bag with me, and I go pick up trash." The people who were involved in the Baltimore Cleanup, and even the people who bore witness on social media, they've been inspired. They think to themselves, "I'm one person, but I can, in my local community and my environment, I can do my part to Make America Great Again." It's the mindset that has inspired people to clean up decrepit cities like Philadelphia. Even in the face of government malfeasance and stagnation, the people still have power.

The Baltimore Cleanup even changed the direction of

Baltimore. After we cleaned up Baltimore, Mayor Brandon Scott announced the Charm City Cleanup Initiative. The initiative combines government services with community volunteer work. "It takes every single one of us doing our part to make sure Baltimore is the cleanest and healthiest she can be, every single day," proclaimed Mayor Scott. "Cleanup is an opportunity for all Baltimoreans to roll up their sleeves and show love to their neighborhoods. As always, I'll be participating, and I look forward to seeing everybody out there doing their part." It's funny how Mayor Scott is now acting like us. No one saw him at our cleanup!

I suppose the old saying is true: *if you can't beat them, join them.*

That's the power of positive action.

It's one thing to critique politicians like Governor Gavin Newscum (to again use President Trump's nickname) and Mayor Brandon Scott, our new Captain Planet (that's my nickname for him). I believe these politicians should be critiqued. But criticism can only go so far. You have to give the people an example of what an alternative looks like. You have to give them a model, something to believe in. We did that in Baltimore, and in Los Angeles, and in other cities across the United States. That's why those cities got cleaned. And that's why people continue to keep those cities clean today. It's also why the Make America Great Again movement only continues to grow. The people are realizing which side of the political spectrum is making our country great again.

The mindset that has always guided my work is the mindset that change is not something in the future. Change is something that you can create *today*. If I want a clean city, I can start that process *today*. If I want safe sidewalks for my children to walk down, I can start that process *today.* If I want my neighborhood to feel like home—a safe and secure home—I don't need to wait for the next election. I've said it a million times, and I will no doubt say it again: be the change you want to see in the world. Don't just sit on the sidelines. Get in the arena and play your part. As the late, great President Theodore Roosevelt put it in his speech at the Sorbonne in Paris on April 23, 1910:

> It is not the critic who counts: not the man who points out how the strong man stumbles or where the doer of deeds could have done better. The credit belongs to the man who is actually in the arena, whose face is marred by dust and sweat and blood, who strives valiantly, who errs and comes up short again and again, because there is no effort without error or shortcoming, but who knows the great enthusiasms, the great devotions, who spends himself in a worthy cause; who, at the best, knows, in the end, the triumph of high achievement, and who, at the worst, if he fails, at least he fails while daring greatly, so that his place shall never be with those cold and timid souls who knew neither victory nor defeat.

For decades, the American people have watched as their freedoms and their God-given rights have been taken from them by the Democratic Party. They have watched as their cities have been taken over by Antifa, and Black Lives Matter, and other radical groups. In TR's words, they have been sitting in the stands of the arena—criticizing, but not acting. Now, there are millions of us in the arena—not only working to get politicians like President

Trump elected and reelected but working hard every day cleaning up our communities and electing local leaders.

While President Trump is fighting for us in the Oval Office, there are millions of us fighting for America on the streets of Baltimore, Los Angeles, and other cities. The arena, we now know, is everywhere. This is what the America First movement is all about. This is what the Make America Great Movement is all about. This is what the most important presidency in American history—Trump's second term in office—is all about.

Remember that permit we requested? The permit we were told we were required to get. After the cleanup was over, the city government sent us an email. They denied us the permit. They denied us the permit after we had already cleaned up their city. If you're still confused about the state that Baltimore is in, just consider that. There's a reason that Donald Trump increasingly appeals to Americans across the political aisle, Americans like the people in Baltimore who have to live under a government that doesn't put their needs first, a government that gets to decide whether you're allowed to remove a dead rat from a children's playground. "The best view of big government," proclaimed President Ronald Reagan, "is in the rearview mirror as we leave it behind."

The best view of a Democratic government, I realized as I drove home to Virginia, is also in the rearview mirror.

Through those campaigns in Baltimore, and in Los Angeles, and in other cities, I also realized that politics is about meeting people where they are. Where do they live? What are their everyday concerns? How can you address their concerns? In short, how can you show up? The best activists, and the best politicians, are people who show up. They show up not to realize their own interests, but to realize the interests of the people they want to serve.

That's what we did in Baltimore. That's what we did in L.A. That is what we did in Philly. We didn't show up to tell people who they should vote for, or who they should leave behind, or who will save their cities. We just showed up and asked what they needed done. And then we did it. Actions speak louder than words. As the old creative writing adage goes: *show, don't tell.*

We showed the people in Kenosha what the America First movement is all about after their city had been destroyed by Antifa.

We showed San Francisco what the America First movement is all about after their city had been neglected for years by Democratic leaders like Nancy Pelosi and Gavin Newsom.

We showed everyone watching around the world—on Twitter, on YouTube, on Facebook, on Rumble, on Truth Social, and on other platforms—what the America First movement is all about.

Above all, we showed people that we didn't care if they voted for a Democrat, or a Republican, or even a socialist—we were in their city to help.

My favorite message to get on social media is the liberal who goes, "Scott, I hate everything about you, but I love your cleanups." I love getting those messages because it means I have chipped the clink in their armor. Even if it's a small chip, I have broken through. And if I break through once, I can break through twice. And if I can break through twice, I can—and will—continue to break through.

Our lord and savior Jesus Christ was said to be a fisher of men. In Matthew 4:19, it is written that He said, "Follow Me, and I will make you fishers of men." When we cleaned up Baltimore, we too were fishers of men. People came out of their homes to help us. They spread that good spirit to others. People who might never have considered voting for President Trump were seeing through the lies of NBC and CNN. They were seeing the truth.

I see myself as part of that great Christian tradition of truth seeking and truth telling, which has found its home in the Republican Party. I'm fishing for Americans to save this country from the untruths, the devastation and the destruction, and, ultimately, from the Left. They can deny us our cleanup passes, and paint us as villains, but the truth never dies. "Blessed are those who are persecuted for righteousness' sake, for theirs is the kingdom of heaven."

Even though they hate me, and even though they despise me, and even though they think President Trump is one of the four horsemen of the apocalypse—they call it the Trumpocalypse—many of these same progressives also respect me. They know I'm not a clicktivist. They know I'm not here to sow division. They know I mean what I say and say what I mean. They know I genuinely care about Making America Great Again. You can't buy respect. You have to earn respect.

It's respect that has catapulted me from two hundred followers, to two thousand followers, to twenty thousand followers, to two hundred thousand followers, to more than two million followers. These days, it's common for people from across the country to DM me. They'll write, "Scott, if you come to San Antonio, I'll help you." Or "Scott, you need to get down to Sante Fe, it's a mess." They'll flood my inbox with messages like, "We're all ready for you in Boston, Scott. The Democrats have turned this city into a dump." Obviously, I'm honored that people from all around the United States reach out to me. But at the same time, I'm not an icon. I'm not anyone special. I'm just an ordinary guy who has taken extraordinary action.

So I'll write back to these people, "You know, I'm so glad to have your help, but start without me! Start tomorrow. Start now." So what if I'm not out there? What's stopping you from picking up that pile of tires in the abandoned lot? What's stopping you from picking up the beer cans near the playground where the neighborhood kids play? What's stopping you from using X, and Instagram, and Facebook, and Truth Social, and Rumble, and all these other wonderful tools to organize the San Antonio Cleanup, or the Sante Fe Cleanup, or the Boston Cleanup? I'm not just trying to sound humble. Every single person has the power to do what I did.

They just need to start.

There's a great quote from Jocko Willink, who commanded SEAL Team Three's Task Unit Bruiser during the battle of Ramadi: "do it and it's done."

That's the mindset that cleans up cities.

That's the mindset that wins elections.

That's the mindset that saves America.

If I were a Democrat, I would be celebrated by the mainstream media establishment. I would be on the cover of the *New York Times*. I would be on CNN every night. I would have a cushy gig in the Democratic National Committee. I would be David Hogg. But because I'm a conservative, because I don't support open borders, the defunding of the police, and socialist health care, those gated communities are closed to me. To even get a DM from a liberal that isn't full of hate, I have to work a hundred times as hard. But guess what? I will always work hard for myself, my team, the Republican Party, and this country. Hard work pays off. You get what you put in. That's the lesson I've learned out there on the streets, and it's the lesson that countless other political activists have learned before me.

Remember Miss Louise?

She was a Democrat.

After we had visited her several times, you know what she said to me?

"No more blue."

That's what reaping the fruits of your labor looks like. That's what change looks like. That's what winning looks like. That's what makes me hopeful about the future of this country.

You can only sell the American people fake news for so long. The beauty of today is that we don't need institutions like the *New York Times* and CNN. With this device in my pocket, I can show the American people what the Make America Great Again movement is doing in cities like Baltimore. I can show the American people what it means to put America First.

And the American people, they are watching.

Between 2020 and 2024, Donald Trump gained millions of voters. That's not luck. That's the result of his hard work and the hard work of all his supporters across the United States, from San Francisco to Boston, who are working hard for him and for this country. Under President Trump's second administration, our movement is only going to get stronger—and the United States of America is only going to get better.

President Trump called it:

> We're going to win. We're going to win so much. We're going to win at trade, we're going to win at the border. We're going to win so much, you're going to be so sick and tired of winning, you're going to come to me and go, "Please, please, we

> can't win anymore." You've heard this one. You'll say, "Please, Mr. President, we beg you sir, we don't want to win anymore. It's too much. It's not fair to everybody else." And I'm going to say, "I'm sorry, but we're going to keep winning, winning, winning. We're going to make America great again."

Our president could not have been more right. We are winning. And—mark my words—we are going to continue to win. We are going to win bigger and better than ever before. The days of Sleepy Joe Biden, Barack Hussein Obama, and the crooked Clintons are over. As the polls show, the influence of the Democrats is waning. As the *NYT* itself acknowledged in an August 2025 headline, "How Democrats Lost Working-Class Voters." Under President's Trump's leadership, a new golden age for America's working class is here. The golden age of America is *finally* here.

We're going to keep winning, winning, and winning.

In the end, the Baltimore Cleanup changed the direction of my life. At the time, I had 250,000 followers on X. Within a year, I had six hundred thousand followers. Within two years, I had nearly one million followers. Now I have more than two million followers. I write this not to pat myself on the back or to sound egotistical. Rather, I want everyone to realize that others will join you when you burn brightly. Again, I want every person that reads this book to firmly understand the power of one—the power in action.

To this day, I'm still known as Scott the Garbage Guy. I'm still known as Scott the Rubbish Dude. If the liberals have Al Gore and Greta Thunberg, the conservatives have Scott the Trash Man. It's my nickname. It's my moniker. It's my sobriquet. I've embraced it. From the east coast to the west coast, and every state in between, I'm known as the Republican who isn't afraid to get his hands dirty. I even lovingly joke about returning home with my parents after the Baltimore cleanup and saying, "Ma, I'm really good at picking up trash."

As I reflected on my time in Baltimore, Los Angeles, San Francisco, Philadelphia, Washington, and other cities controlled by the Democratic Party, I was left with a question that wasn't just burned into my brain, but it was a question that was also burned into my heart and soul: How do we stop their reign of terror? To put it differently, if the Democrats continued to be elected to office, our movement would only be pouring water on a roaring fire that continued to be fanned by their disastrous policies.

With these great American city cleanups in my rearview mirror, I knew where my next battle for the future of the United States would take me.

It would take me to the voting booth.

CHAPTER 3

GET OUT THE VOTE

While the Baltimore Cleanup opened my eyes to the power of grassroots activism, it also left me unfulfilled. Yes, hundreds of us had united. Yes, we had removed twelve tons of trash from the city. Yes, the city was safer for children after we left. We could come back to Charm City every month. Heck, we could come back every week. But at the end of the day, we weren't in power. The Democrats were in power. The problem of criminal illegal aliens stealing affordable housing, driving down wages, and catapulting Baltimoreans into homelessness—that problem was going to continue, and get worse, if the Democrats stayed in power. Moreover, the Democrats had the power in cities across the United States. To put it simply, I realized that if we only continued to clean up after the Democrats, quite literally, then America would never be great again. As I drove home to Virginia after the Baltimore Cleanup, I knew what we had to do. I didn't just want to be a Band-Aid—I wanted to help deliver long-term solutions.

We had to win elections.

Voter registration has been on my mind since 2013. Back then, I was volunteering for Ken Cuccinelli. He was running for Virginia governor against Terry McAuliffe. McAuliffe beat Cuccinelli. He then used his executive power to pardon more than two hundred thousand convicted felons. This was right before the 2016 election. That November, Hillary Clinton defeated Donald Trump. She edged out a victory by about 200,000 votes in Virginia. But it wasn't just that election that made me fixate on voter registration. I was aware of the data. From 2008, to 2012, and then to 2016, the Republican vote margin had been stagnant. It was about 1.7, 1.7, and 1.7. Republicans weren't growing. They were following the same playbook in a commonwealth that was steadily slipping out of their grasp. Democrats were evolving and devising new ways to flip states from red to blue, while Republicans were stuck in the past. The Democrats had registered hundreds of thousands of new voters going into the 2008 election. While Virginians had elected George W. Bush in 2000 and 2004, the Democrats—buttressed by a growing army of new voters—defeated the GOP in 2008, 2012, and 2016.

It was clear: voter registration matters.

There are so many aspects of American politics that are fun, and exciting, and even a little bit sexy. Have you seen the beautiful MAGA influencers on Instagram? Did you see the photographs from the "America Is Hot Again" event at Butterworth's? Even the *Washington Post*, that beacon of misinformation, couldn't help but acknowledge the truth: "in Trump's Washington, MAGA fashionistas lay claim to American hotness." Indeed, there are a lot of things to get excited about in American politics, especially if you're part of the America First movement. There are rallies. There are parties. There's going to be a UFC event on the White House lawn. But voter registration isn't one of the things people get excited about. When Republicans think about voter registration—if they even think about it at all—they think of a fold-up table inside a high school gymnasium.

Historically, the Democratic Party has controlled the voter registration movement. Not only have they controlled it, they have utterly dominated it. I mean, really, just look at the titles of videos and articles. "Democrats Post Big Gains in Voter Registration." "Democrats Launch Massive Voter Registration Drive to Turn Texas Blue." "DSA's Campaign: Voter Registration Drive in New York." "Gillum, Florida Democrats Launch Massive Voter Registration Drive Ahead of 2020." In that video, Andrew Gillum proclaims to his audience: "Are ya'll ready to flip the United States of America blue?" In 2016, Hillary Clinton won 65,853,514 votes. In 2020, Joe Biden won 81,283,501 votes. Of note, Trump gained more than 10 million more votes between these two elections. But that wasn't enough. Clearly, the Democratic Party's monumental and nationwide effort to register new voters paid off.

Most recently, we saw this pay off in New York City. Zohran Mamdani, then a virtual nobody, beat the former governor of New York, Andrew Cuomo. Given that Cuomo was the Democratic National Committee's preferred candidate, Mamdani's landslide win was all the more impressive. How did State Assemblyman Mamdani beat the former governor? What made the difference? According to the *New York Times*, "Mr. Mamdani changed the electoral map. In the 14 days leading up to the registration deadline for the Democratic primary, about 37,000 people registered to vote, compared with about 3,000 people in the same period in 2021 . . . Mr. Mamdani's campaign had focused on registering voters, and he also appears to have drawn thousands of voters to the primary who did not vote four years ago." In short, socialist Mamdani knows how to win elections.

Importantly, Mamdani showed up in the communities where he knew he would find support. "Mr. Mamdani boosted turnout among new voters in Muslim and South Asian neighborhoods. Many immigrants saw themselves in the story of Mr. Mamdani, 33, who is Muslim and was born to Indian parents in Uganda." Mamdani also knew how important it was to vote early, so did the people who were out registering new voters on his behalf. In the Greenpoint neighborhood in Brooklyn, their "neighborhood had one of the highest shares of early voters who supported Mr. Mamdani and did not vote in the 2021 mayoral primary. On some blocks, more than 80 percent of voters backed him." I'll say it again: Mamdani might be a bozo when it comes to policies, but he is not a bozo when it comes to winning elections. He and the socialists who support him know how to win elections.

The problem is that many Republicans—that is, those who have the policies that America needs—don't know how to win elections. Instead of paralleling the Democrats' enormous success with voter registration and early voting, they have sat on the sidelines. Some Republicans don't even believe in voting; they believe the system is too rigged to be saved, and they believe their vote won't matter, if it's even counted at all. That really became the case after the 2020 election. Other Republicans believe early voting is especially tainted and prone to malfeasance. I share their concerns. But I'm also a pragmatist. If there's a tool on the table, every Republican needs to pick it up and use it. We must fight fire with a gosh darn flamethrower. Voter registration drives and early voting are wonderfully effective tools—as Mamdani the Commie, to use President Trump's nickname, and his gang of socialists know.

They also know that the voter registration movement has long been controlled by their side of the aisle.

In the weeks leading up to the 2024 presidential election, that immediately became clear to anyone who wasn't already paying attention. On October 22, 2024, WHAS11 reported that more than 15 million Americans had already voted. Let me write that again: more than 15 million Americans had already voted—and it wasn't even November! Forty-seven percent of those early votes came from Democrats and just 33 percent came from Republicans, found one survey from the *Washington Post* and the Schar School of Policy and Government at George Mason University. According to that survey, early Democratic voters were trouncing early Republican voters in Georgia. They were trouncing early Republican voters in Wisconsin. They were trouncing early Republican voters in Michigan. And they were trouncing early Republican voters in my own state, the beautiful Commonwealth of Pennsylvania.

Do you know how many Electoral College votes Georgia has? Sixteen. Do you know how many Wisconsin has? Ten. Do you know how many Michigan has? Fifteen. What about Pennsylvania? Nineteen. Just these four states represent sixty Electoral College votes. Let me write that again: sixty Electoral College votes. Equally important, these are swing states. On the eve of the election, the BBC reported that just seven swing states, including these four, could decide the 2024 US election. And guess what? The Democrats were absolutely trouncing the Republicans when it came to early votes. From the beginning, the Democrats were in it to win it.

If you are a pragmatist and you're in this to win elections for the Republican Party, those numbers should be terrifying. They should keep you up at night, tossing and turning, and thinking about the question that I am always thinking about: How do we become the party that votes early and votes often? To become that party we have to confront the enormous apparatus that has ensured that the Democrats always dominate voter registration drives and mail-in ballot drives. I call it the Democratic Voting Industrial Complex. The DVIC is well-funded, well-organized, and it never sleeps. From presidential elections to midterms, it is one of the beasts that keeps the Democratic Party not only alive but thriving.

It's buttressed by the so-called nonpartisan, nonprofit organizations.

It's funny, even the voter registration initiatives that purport to be nonpartisan, and which have a tax-exempt status because they purport to be nonpartisan, look like Democratic National Committee initiatives. Just watch Rock the Vote's short 2012 video entitled "History of Voting!" "Based on this video," reports the *Washington Examiner*, "one would think voting Republican is like electing your own tyrants to dominate you, voluntarily bonding yourself, sacrificing the liberties of your well-meaning gay friends, consciously destroying the planet, and facing a death the equivalent to being smashed by the spiked pillars of a U.S. Army tank—likely one driven by a heartless soulless skeleton, as is featured in this video." Two of the celebrities in the video, John Legend and Darren Criss, have both performed at Barack Obama fundraisers. In plain English, Rock the Vote, like so many other get-out-the-vote initiatives, have not let their tax-exempt, non-profit status interfere with their political work for the Democratic Party.

More recently, the Democrats have exploited social unrest. "In 2020," writes Joshua Douglas, "after the murder of George Floyd and the ensuing protests on police brutality, voter registration surged, at least among Democrats and independents. The protests themselves served as voter registration opportunities: one report noted that activists placed QR codes to voter registration websites on their protest signs so people could scan the code on their phones." While Republicans were trying to protect cities like Los Angeles, Minneapolis, and Kenosha from burning to the ground, the Democrats were using these public safety emergencies to expand their voter registration lists. As Rahm Emanuel, the former mayor of Chicago and chief of staff to President Barack Obama, so eloquently put it: "you never want a serious crisis to go to waste."

While I think Rahm Emmanuel is as morally broken as they come, even a broken clock is right twice a day.

Right now, there are innumerable crises in the United States. There's the crisis of homelessness. There's the crisis at our southern border. There's the crisis of free speech and the Left's censorship of every perspective with which it disagrees. There's the crisis of men taking over women's sports. There's the crisis of radical Islamic terrorism. In Iraq, Afghanistan, and other countries, Muslims chant "death to America!" There's the crisis of Iran building a nuclear weapon. There's the crisis of China taking over the global economy. There's the crisis of mandatory vaccinations and the enormous power wielded by the pharmaceutical industry. There's the crisis of the liberal media, which has entirely abandoned anything even vaguely resembling journalistic standards. There's the crisis of the deep state, which is doing everything in its power to stop the America First movement. As Howard Beale puts it in his famous monologue from the film *Network*, "we know things are bad, worse than bad."

Comrade Zohran Mamdani understands this as well as anyone

on the Left. He understands that homelessness is a problem in NYC. He understands that New Yorkers are struggling to survive on minimum wage jobs. He understands that rent is really, really expensive—and that it will continue to go up. But the "solutions" that he proposes, like rent control and a minimum wage of $30 an hour, are only going to make these problems worse—much worse. It's not just the problem of landlords being hurt. It's not just the problem of businesses fleeing NYC to find more hospitable climates. It's the problem of AI being brought in to replace the minimum wage workers who business owners, especially the small business owners who make NYC great, will no longer be able to afford to pay when the minimum wage skyrockets to $30 an hour.

As Santiago Vidal Calvo reflects, "In 2024, when California set a new $20 minimum wage for fast-food workers—a 25% hike—many operators raced to automate their restaurants. Within a month of the increase, one franchisee for LA's El Pollo Loco said she bought two kiosks for each of her stores at about $25,000 per location, after calculating the new $20-an-hour wages would cost her an extra $180,000 annually at every restaurant. Workers ultimately lost out there, and the same pattern could emerge in Gotham."

But, as I have said before and I will no doubt say again, Mayor Mamdani understands the people who live in his city. These are their concerns: housing and wages. And he has built a platform that purports to address their concerns. More than that, he has built the voter movement to get him into power. This is the movement of voter registration as well as the movement of early voting. What Mamdani and his team lack in policies, they make up for in their rhetorical appeals to the real concerns of New Yorkers as well as their on-the-ground tactical strategies, which have long been ignored by the Right.

The Democrats, despite their morally broken compass, have been incredibly effective. Time and time again, they have taken advantage of crises. They have used crises to register new voters. They have been able to turn purple states blue. They have even been able to turn red states blue. I'm a pragmatist. When the Democrats are successful, I study their tactics. I steal their tactics. And I make those tactics better. What the Democrats were able to do to in Virginia, a red state that was all in for George W. Bush in 2000 and 2004, was regrettable. But it was also incredible. For those of us on the Right who were paying close attention, the Democratic Party had given us the blueprint.

At the end of the day, I don't care where a blueprint comes from. It could come from Rahm Emannuel. It could come from Zohran Mandani. It could come from Anderson Cooper. It could even come from Jim Dandeneau, executive director of the Vermont Democratic Party, who once said of me, "this is not someone who has any business being celebrated by a responsible political party and this is not someone who should be welcome in Vermont." It really doesn't matter. Every morning when I wake up, whether I'm at my home in Pennsylvania, or I'm in a hotel because I'm on the road registering new voters, I have one goal in my mind: turn all of the United States red.

This is because I don't want to see America become the next Soviet Union. I don't want to see New York City turn into Los Angeles, San Francisco, or Portland. I don't want to see more people evicted from their homes, kicked out of their jobs, and otherwise catapulted into financial ruin. I most certainly don't want to see politicians come to power who are intent on dividing the

American people and alienating our allies abroad. What I see in the antisemitism and socialism of radical left-wing politicians like Communist Mamdani isn't the end of heartache, but the end of America.

The stakes right now—to win elections—could not be higher.

The Beginning

Back in 2019, I was invited to lead my first voter registration event. I was invited up to Kent, a small town in Litchfield County, Connecticut. The event was part of the #Trump2020 campaign. This was the Constitution State. This was the state where great Republicans like United States Secretary of Education Linda McMahon lived. It was also a blue state. In 2004, they voted for John Kerry. In 2008, they voted for Barack Obama. In 2012, they voted for Obama again. In 2016, Connecticut belonged to Hillary Clinton. But there were hundreds of thousands of people who had voted for Donald Trump. I believed this was a state we could win. And I could not have been more excited to travel there.

On the one hand, the Democrats claim to be the defenders of democracy. According to their rhetoric, they want everyone to vote. They want everyone to have a voice. Also, according to them, Donald Trump is a fascist who must be silenced. Moreover, all of his allies and supporters must be silenced too. The Left is for voting, as long as you're voting for their preferred candidates. The Left is for free speech, as long as it's the freedom to speak positively about their party.

In the Left's eyes, all of Donald Trump's supporters are a basket of deplorables. They are either immoral or stupid. Often, they are depicted as immoral *and* stupid. They're looked down upon for supporting the GOP. They're looked down upon for being

Christian. They're looked down upon for working with their hands. They're looked down upon for still believing there are only two genders. Moreover, they are the harbingers of doom—little better than the so-called mindless masses who pushed Adolph Hitler into power on August 19, 1934, when he was elected president of Germany.

"Voters elected Hitler because they liked his fascist promise. Trump's reelection repeats that history," writes University of Illinois Urbana-Champaign professor Peter Fritzsche.

"Hundreds of scholars say U.S. is swiftly heading toward authoritarianism," reports NPR.

As Bernie Sanders said of President Trump, "he's usurping the powers of the United States Congress. This guy wants all of the power. He does not believe in the constitution. He does not believe in the rule of law."

In this narrative, pushed by the DNC, and the universities, and the liberal media outlets, the Democrats are the only people standing in the way of the absolute and utter destruction of our constitution. They are the only ones standing in the way of the absolute and utter destruction of our liberties, freedoms, and rights. In short, they are the only ones standing in the way of a full-blown authoritarian, neo-fascist, fourth Reich state. Raise the alarms! Blow the horns! The Trumpocalypse is right on the horizon!

At a recent event in California, while I was writing this book, representative Jared Huffman declared that the United States is "speed walking toward authoritarianism." A young woman in his audience added, "I am watching history repeat itself. Donald Trump and his enablers are not just political opponents, they are a threat to democracy." This woman compared Donald Trump's return to the White House to Adolph Hitler's rise to power in Germany. She received a standing ovation.

When the other side is treated as "not just political opponents," but "a threat to democracy," violence is the only rational response.

It's this radical thinking that has provoked the attempts to assassinate President Trump.

It's this radical thinking that provoked the assassination of Charlie Kirk.

On the other hand, the Democrats have tightly controlled voter registrations drives forever—to their advantage. They do not want conservative Americans to get to the polls. They understand how critically important voter registration drives are to the outcomes of federal, state, and local elections. The Democrats do not care about voting as an end in itself. The more people who vote for them—legally or not—is all the Democrats care about. And they will do everything in their power to keep conservatives out of the United States voting booths.

When I traveled down to Kent, Connecticut, to lead an event where I could teach people how to get out the vote, the local Democrats did not welcome me with open arms. They did not applaud me for trying to increase the number of people in our county who vote. They did not cheer me and my team for trying to increase Democratic participation in their state. Instead, they showed their true colors. These Democrats, they were absolutely infuriated.

"We have not succeeded in getting tomorrow's Scott Presler event canceled," proclaimed a Facebook post from the Kent Democratic Town Committee. "I know it is disappointing. But, the die is cast and we must move on." How did they "move on"? They announced plans to protest my event. Remember: I wasn't

Antifa or the DSA. I wasn't there to do anything radical. I was there to help people get out the vote. In the Left's eyes, that makes me a threat. That makes me someone who needs to be cancelled. In an interesting twist of irony, the very people calling President Trump and his supporters fascist tried to cancel me and ended up protesting me because they disagreed with my free speech. It was my first voter registration training and my first protest—a badge of honor.

In America, if you are a Republican who wants to register voters, you have to confront the juggernaut of the Democratic Party establishment. You have to confront the fringe radical socialists who want to see the voting booths filled only with people who will vote for their candidates. In short, you have to confront The Resistance. In the eyes of The Resistance, the only thing that matters is your obedience to the Democratic Party.

Remember: this is the party that didn't let their own constituency vote for a candidate to run in the 2024 presidential election.

To their own voters, they said: "Keep your mouth shut. There will be no primaries. Kamala Harris is your choice." This is the party that was so committed to democracy it had a barely conscious marionette in the Oval Office for four years while Democratic Party insiders, who no one voted into office, pulled the strings and reshaped the direction of the United States federal government. Even Jake Tapper, the lead Washington anchor for CNN, couldn't help but acknowledge the truth in his book *Original Sin: President Biden's Decline, Its Cover-Up, and His Disastrous Choice to Run Again*. What the Democrats did was "part of a larger act of extended public deception that has few precedents." This is the party that purports to protect democracy. This is the party that claims to safeguard election integrity. This is the party that says it's protecting us from "the rising threat of fascism on the Right."

Just look at what the Democratic Party did to Bernie Sanders. Sanders, who has been highly critical of the millionaires and billionaires who fund establishment Democrats like Hillary Clinton and Barack Obama, has been a perpetual target of the Left. Donald Trump hit the nail on the head in a July 2016 tweet after a Wikileaks release: "Leaked e-mails of DNC show plans to destroy Bernie Sanders. Mock his heritage and much more. On-line from Wikileakes, really vicious. RIGGED." The Democrats not only want to prevent Republicans like me from registering voters; they want to prevent people within their party's fringes from gaining power. In short, they want to very tightly control who their own voters can vote for.

They shouldn't be called the Democratic Party, they should be called the democrat party (that's what I call them on social media)—because there's nothing democratic about what they did to Bernie.

This is not the party in George Orwell's *1984*.

This is the Democratic Party in the United States of America.

The Democrats love democracy as much as United States Secretary of Health and Human Services Robert F. Kennedy Jr. loves sugar, McDonald's, and Red No. 3

This is why I wasn't surprised when I got the news that Democrats were planning to protest my event in Connecticut. What? Scott Presler is trying to increase the amount of people who participate in our elections? What's that? Scott Presler wants more Americans to have a say over who their future leaders are? Are you serious? He's going to be in our state, giving the American people the tools they need to not only preserve, but expand our democracy? I don't believe it! That's an emergency! Assemble the troops! Let's shut him down!

"Hey, hey, ho, ho, Scott Presler has got to go!"

"Hey, hey, ho, ho, Scott Presler has got to go!"

"Hey, hey, ho, ho, Scott Presler has got to go!"

That's the Democrats' strategy. Shut down the event. Slander the person in the media. Make sure they are discredited and silenced. "Virginian linked to hate group will hold 'activism' seminar in New Milford," reported the *CT Post*. If all that doesn't work, then just pull the trigger—as the Left did to Charlie Kirk.

Again, I wasn't heading to Connecticut to protest President Joe Biden. I wasn't heading there to attack the local Democratic politicians. I was heading there to talk about voting—you know, the process that keeps our democracy alive. That is why I was a threat. That is why I was marked as a target. That is why I had to be neutralized.

As I was preparing for my trip, I wasn't particularly thrilled to hear there would be protests. But that didn't mean I was going to stoop to their level. "I do hear that they are going to have protests from the Western Socialists of Connecticut for little old me," I said in a Facebook video, "but that's okay because I'm bringing love, and I'm so excited to be in your state. And I cannot wait to teach you the art of voter registration." Michelle Obama famously said, "when they go low, we go high." Democrats talk the talk. But Republicans walk the walk. My motto is, "when they go low, we go to the polls."

The event in Kent, Connecticut, was a resounding success. For my first event, we had over one hundred attendees; some even came from New York. With a projector and screen, I gave a PowerPoint presentation on what most people think is a boring topic: voter registration. Armed with humor and anecdotes, I landed jokes and began what I like to think of as focus groups. Just like President Trump, I am constantly testing messaging. If I tell a joke a few times and it doesn't get laughs, it gets cut. Every interaction with people is an opportunity to learn and hone my skills.

The Connecticut event brought moms, dads, families, and some even brought their dogs. We were prepared with signs and even took a group photo at the end showing the diversity of the crowd. Despite the Democrats trying to ruin the day, it was a ten out of ten. Little did I know, this one event in a small state would turn into a tour across the country and lead to tens of thousands of new registered Republicans.

By the time I left, those beautiful residents of Connecticut had the tools they needed to get out the vote. They also had a fire lit inside of them. That November after I left town, Joe Biden barely etched out a win over Donald Trump and Mike Pence in Litchfield County. We were just 118 votes short of a victory. It's those close margins that worry the Kent Democratic Town Committee and other Democratic committees in counties across the United States. That's why they wanted to shut down my event. That's why they want to retain total control over the voter registration movement. They want it to remain the voter registration movement for Democrats.

But the Republican voter registration movement is growing. From the east coast to the west coast, and every state in between, I'm seeing the effects of our work. Countless counties that have long been blue—including counties that Republicans didn't even believe could turn purple—are now turning red. I call it the *reddening of America*. And I could not be more excited to play my part in this America First revolution.

As Ulysses S. Grant said, "The right of revolution is an inherent one. When people are oppressed by their government, it is a natural right they enjoy to relieve themselves of the oppression."

Could you imagine a better description of the Make America Great Again movement?

After Connecticut, I started traveling the country. I told all my followers on social media—two hundred thousand at the time—that I would meet them wherever they were. I didn't ask for a $20,000 speaking fee ("socialist" Cornel West charges $20,000 plus travel expenses). I didn't ask to be put up in a five-star hotel with a hot tub and a mini bar. I didn't ask to have a chauffeur take me from my hotel to my events. That's not what I am about. I didn't even ask for a speaking fee. I didn't ask for an honorarium. In all honesty, I didn't ask for any money. I was blunt and to the point. I said, "if you find me a place to sleep, I'll be there."

That's what this movement is all about.

Action. Action. And more action.

If you want fame and big paychecks, there's other career paths for you.

A grassroots activist is in the grassroots.

Never did I think this would be my life. If you told me that I would be traveling the country registering voters and picking up trash, I would have told you that you bumped your head and lost your mind. There are moments when I'm tired and I find myself struggling to continue going, but I think of all the people that have welcomed me into their homes. Literally, hundreds of families have opened their hearts and houses to me. It's always an honor when a family makes this offer because it means I've earned their trust and respect. As an added bonus, I usually get to cuddle with their animals. In fact, some supporters will even tell me they have cuddly dogs almost in an attempt to get me to stay with them. In my introductions, injecting the universal language of humor, I'll often say at events: "People invite me into their homes. I cuddle with their animals." Pause. "It's another thing when the owner tries to cuddle with you." This punchline always elicits laughter without fail. Of course this hasn't happened, but it's my goal to entertain as much as it is to inform at these voter registration events. From studying President Trump and his ability to elevate conversations, I use humor and personality to make elections fun.

Traveling the country, registering tens of thousands of voters, and helping Republicans turn their counties red, that's what I did from 2019 through 2022. From sunrise to sundown, that was my life. I ate, slept, and breathed politics. Votes, votes, and more votes. It didn't matter where I was. I was in it to win it.

When people call me The Persistence, it's that attitude they have in mind. The attitude of getting the job done—no matter what. I'll hop on a flight, a bus, a train, or in my former 2005 Honda Civic (thank you, Aunt Rose & Uncle Ray) to go and get the job done. Wherever voters are, that's where I am heading. And guess what? That attitude is contagious.

Just as social media helped me connect with people who hosted me for voter registration events, those events also increased the number of people who followed me on social media. By the end of 2022, I had 1.3 million followers. It was clear that there was an enormous and up until this point untapped conservative audience for Republican voter registration efforts.

People were excited. They were hopeful. They understood

what I was doing. They understood how important it was to the future of the Grand Old Party—and the future of this country. They understood the need to vote early and the need to vote often. They understood that this is what makes the difference. This is what makes the difference between a city that is crumbling from violence and homelessness, like Governor Gavin Newsom's San Francisco, and a city that is thriving now more than ever, like Governor Ron DeSantis's Miami. Above all, they understood that is the difference between another Make America Great Again presidency or four more years of Sleepy Joe Biden.

More and more, the Republican pundits and strategists—not just the rank and file—were recognizing that even though voter registration had long been the terrain of the Democratic Party, it didn't need to be their terrain any longer. In fact, it didn't need to be that way much longer. They were recognizing that the tide was turning and that certain individuals, including me, were provoking a red wave of voter registration efforts across the United States of America.

It was also clear that I had become a leader—if not *the* leader—in this growing voter registration and early voting movement on the Right. I had gone from looking at George W. Bush's photograph in my parents' kitchen as a kid, to getting involved in Greg Abbott's reelection campaign, to leading the new voting movement of America First Republicans putting politicians like Donald Trump into office. As I joked in that social media post, the Democrats were now protesting little old me: the guy who used to be a dog walker!

My journey has been thrilling, but it has also been surreal. I have never desired fame. My grandfather was a military veteran. My father is a military veteran. I come from a long line of men who value service over status. I would feel just as fulfilled if I was working as a border patrol agent. I would feel just as fulfilled if I deleted my X account tomorrow. I enjoy social media. I have fun with it. But I don't seek stardom. To the extent that a large social media platform helps me achieve concrete political victories in the real world, that's what I care about.

But the more voters I registered between 2019 and 2022, the more quickly it became apparent that I was becoming a star in conservative politics. My star was rising not because I had a hit podcast, not because I had a column in *National Review*, not because I have luxurious long hair (though, let's not kid ourselves, these locks have played a part), and not because I'm a little nepo baby whose parents paved the road for me. Hi Chelsea Clinton!

My star was rising because I was putting in the work, day after day, week after week, month after month, and year after year. It didn't matter if it was a Thursday morning in Philadelphia or a Sunday evening in San Francisco, I had my boots on the ground. Persistence is a Presler family value. It always has been. It always will be. Persistence, as everyone in my family knows, it pays off. When it comes to my political work, my core value is persistence. Why? Persistence is what gets results. Results, that's what I care about the most.

Recently, a friend put it in perspective for me. He said, "Scott, just stop for a moment and think about it. You get phone calls from Steve Bannon. Elon Musk has retweeted you more than once. You were just on Fox News. Lara Trump tells everyone about the important work you do. That's a political mastermind, the richest man in the world, a major television network, and the daughter of the president of the United States of America. Not that long ago, you were picking up dog droppings. Scott, that is unbelievable."

I'm grateful for the life that I have created. It was love that got me here. I have love for freedom. I have love for liberty. I have love for this country. I have love for the Republican Party because I believe they are the only party that can save this country. I also love playing my part in the Republican revolution. You don't have to spend more than three seconds on my social media to see that I love registering voters to fight for the Grand Old Party.

"From as early as I can remember, my father would say to me, 'The most important thing in life is to love what you're doing, because that's the only way you'll ever be really good at it,'" reflects Donald Trump in *The Art of the Deal.* Every morning that I wake up, I love fighting for our country and our president's America First agenda.

When I get a call from the president, or from Mr. Bannon, or I have a conversation with Mrs. Lara Trump, or Mr. Musk retweets me, or when I'm in the studio at Fox News, I truly am filled with gratitude. There's nothing more rewarding than being acknowledged by the people you look up to, the people you respect, and people who you aspire to emulate.

At the same time, I don't think my life is an accident. I worked hard. As a result of that hard work, this is the life I live. Above all, this is the life *you* can live. My life really is just an example of what happens when one man decides to take action. It shows what happens when he inspires his fellow Americans to take action, too. While the story of Scott Presler is extraordinary, the origins of that story are ordinary. I write this as respectfully as possible: I am the American dream. Having this realization is what keeps me going. I want everyone to have the opportunity to go from the doghouse to the White House.

At the end of 2022, I knew I had to go bigger. I knew I had to do more. With arguably the most important election in American history less than two years away, I knew that now was the time to launch a new organization, one that would permanently seize the voter registration movement from the Democratic Party.

In January of 2023, I launched Early Vote Action.

Early Vote Action

At EVA, our mission is to register Republican voters and get them committed to vote early, by absentee ballot, by mail, or in person on Election Day—by any means necessary! We are a nationwide group of grassroots activists, volunteers, and paid staff who dedicate their time, resources, and hard work to achieving this goal in the battleground states of Arizona, Michigan, Nevada, New Jersey, North Carolina, Pennsylvania, and Wisconsin.

With the help of Early Vote Action's dedicated volunteers, my team and I have contacted hundreds of thousands of voters since the inception of our organization. Our network, which spans the entire fifty United States and many US territories, is especially focused on winning elections in these critical battleground states. The Democrats have turned a number of purple states blue. We're turning them red.

Using proven methods of voter contact—including handwritten postcards and letters, text messages, phone calls, and, of course, our boots on the ground—the EVA network has dramatically shifted voter registration rolls in counties across the United States in favor of Republicans. Our grassroots network has proven time and time again that, no matter where they live in these great

United States, any motivated conservative American can join the movement to save our country.

So what does EVA's work look like on a day-to-day basis?

There's a lot of political work that doesn't require social skills. You can be behind the scenes writing speeches. You can be fact-checking claims made by political opponents. You can be crunching numbers into an Excel spreadsheet. There's a lot of work that doesn't require you to interact a lot with other people. But in the game of voter registration, you have to be a people person.

I love people. I love audiences. In another world, I might have majored in theater. I'm also someone who is committed to my craft. I'm very confident in my craft. How I talk, how I walk, how I make eye contact, how I smile, how I pause, how I hold the attention of a room full of thousands of people, how I connect with a single individual on the street—none of this is an accident.

There's an expression in the NBA. It's called "taking a game off." Basketball has long seasons. The players play a lot of games. Sometimes a player will show up on the court. But they'll be running a little slower, they'll be jumping a little lower, they'll be taking the game off. They say Michael Jordan never took a game off. It didn't matter if Jordan had the flu—as he did in game five of the 1997 NBA finals, when he scored thirty-eight points—or a broken leg. If you had tickets to a Bulls game, you were going to see Air Jordan. You weren't going to see someone who simply showed up.

That's the mindset I bring to voter registration. It's also the mindset I model for every member of my team. It doesn't matter if I'm jetlagged. It doesn't matter if I've been stuck in my car for twelve hours. It doesn't matter if I'm having a bad hair day. Regardless of how I feel, I bring my best self to every single interaction. It doesn't matter if it's a room full of three thousand people or a room full of three people. If you meet me, you're going to meet me. Like Michael Jordan, I don't take time off. And unlike the NBA, voter registration doesn't have an offseason. Day after day, week after week, month after month, and year after year—there really are no breaks. There's always the next election, and it's always right there on the horizon. From the Oval Office to the state legislatures, I'm in it to win it.

My craft is important to me, and I've refined it over the years. But there's also something to be said about the nature of what I do. Judge Judy says, if you tell the truth, you don't have to lie. She's a smart woman. I like that Judge Judy. She also says, if you tell the truth, you don't have to have a good memory. That's a model for how to live your life. The Democrats love to say they're speaking truth to power. To be frank, I've heard relatively little truth come from that side. But their expression is one to live by. Every day, when I'm out there working hard for the Republican Party, I am speaking truth to power.

Many kids, when they're young, they like to talk a lot. Many of these kids, they're not the best listeners. I think it's a lot more difficult to listen than it is to speak. It's a lot harder to focus your mind, to listen to every word a person says, and to not simply wait for your turn to talk. The biggest thing I have learned from my years of voter registration is this: listen. Really pay attention to what people are saying to you. Be an active listener. That's true whether it's a phone call from Mr. Bannon or a conversation with a homeless man outside a gas station. People want to rush conversations. They want to have their turn. That's not the best approach to register voters. Voters, especially American voters, they want to feel heard.

One of the many things President Trump and I have in common is we love to listen. Trump is known for always asking people what they think, not just the people in his inner circle, but the ordinary Americans he confronts on the campaign trail, in a McDonald's, and on a golf course. There's a reason his policies connect to the interests of so many people—people as different as a Black mother in the Bronx and a college quarterback in Montgomery, Alabama. He listens to what people need, and he builds the policies that deliver. When I'm out there talking to voters, it's that approach that I keep in mind. It's not my job to tell you what you need. It's my job to listen to what you need.

Both President Trump and I, we also know how to hold a room. You've seen videos of his campaign speeches. They're like rock shows. They really are off the charts. He's not just another politician standing in front of a podium, reciting some drab lines from a teleprompter. President Trump, he doesn't speak in a monotone. He doesn't need to pause for a glass of water. He doesn't need any breaks. That energy he brings to each and every event, it's contagious. He knows when to raise his voice. He knows when to take it down a notch. He knows when to get serious. And he knows when a joke, or two, or three, is needed. Unlike Sleepy Joe Biden, this is a president who doesn't put Americans to sleep. The American people, they love that energy. Why? Because they feel how much our president cares.

In the same way Donald Trump has inspired millions of people to travel to the polls for him, I haven't registered tens of thousands of voters because I'm a career politician. I'm not an actor. No one writes my speeches. No one tweets my tweets. I don't have a handler. What you see is what you get. If someone was telling me what to say, and what to write, and when to opine, and when to keep my mouth shut, I wouldn't have half the following I do. Americans, they crave authenticity—and, unfortunately, in many corners of American politics, it's authenticity that is in short supply.

In fact, I think I have been so effective because I don't come from that background. My mom is not a politician. My dad is not a pundit. They taught me values—important ones. But they didn't teach me the decorum of the D.C. swamp. Like Trump, I'm an outsider. I didn't arrive to do business as usual. I entered the scene to shake things up. Instead of trying to follow a playbook, I created my own.

Of course, I've taken pieces of that playbook from other people and from other organizations. As I've mentioned, the Democrats have been enormously effective with their voter registration efforts. But they've also fallen short—especially with certain demographics. Learning from their mistakes, EVA is already becoming the most influential voter registration organization in the United States. I'm proud of that. But it hasn't happened by accident. Few things do.

The core philosophy of EVA's playbook is simple: *meet conservatives where they are*. Who are the people who are most likely to vote for Republican candidates? Where do they pray? Where do they take their children to play? Where do they buy a new truck? Where do they go out to dinner? Where do they work out? Where do they dance the night away? Where do they get their tractor-trailer fixed? Where do they feel like they can speak their mind without punishment? Where do they feel at home?

These are questions that my team and I think about—constantly. We don't set up voter registration booths everywhere and anywhere. We are strategic. And we are targeted. The liberals can have the boutique vegan grocery stores, the Planned Parenthood centers, and the Beyoncé concerts. They can also have the people salivating outside of *The Daily Show* studio, the people running in the Run for Refugees fundraiser, and the people walking into the Brooklyn bookstore that has an "Abolish ICE" poster hanging from its storefront window.

Me and the rest of the EVA team, we set up shop up in the places where we are more likely to find the Americans who share our values—the Americans who share our values, but who are not yet planning to head to the polls to turn these values into policies. Voter registration is, in many ways, the process of giving people the tools they need to build the world they want. Their vote is an invaluable tool.

History is unpredictable. And it affords new opportunities to reshape the political landscape in this country. Lakewood is a beautiful Jewish community in Pennsylvania. There is a gun range there called We Shoot. The Jewish community, now they call it We Vote—and I'll tell you why. After October 7, 2023, guns have been flying off the shelves like bread during the Great Depression. The Jewish community is buying them at extraordinarily high rates. They're exercising their Second Amendment right in a profound way. And you guessed it right; I'm out there making sure that they are also exercising their right to vote.

While we do focus on these spaces where we think we can register conservatives, we also set up shop in places where we know we will find large numbers of people, at least some of whom will share our values. Sometimes we end up in some unique situations. Do you remember the recent solar eclipse? At the time, I was reading about it. But because I'm a voter registration fanatic, I was also thinking about registering voters. What I realized was that the voter registration deadline for the county of Erie had been extended because of the solar eclipse. And Erie, that is the consequential swing county in Pennsylvania. So you know what my team and I did? We drove out there during the eclipse. We got an RV and set up shop in the casino parking lot where everyone in Erie was watching the eclipse. We had a little fun, and we came with a life-size Donald Trump cutout. We even showed up with those little black solar eclipse glasses. You know who wasn't there? The Democrats. And guess what? We got conservative voters registered in the pitch-black shadow of the eclipse.

You know what the headline of GoErie.com was on November 6, 2024? "Former President Donald Trump reclaims Erie County, turning crucial bellwether red again." As they wrote, "Erie lived up to its reputation as one of the country's ultimate bellwether counties in a critical battleground state. On Tuesday, voters here gave former President Donald Trump another razor-thin victory, a nearly identical margin to his 2016 win—just under 2,000 votes—reflecting the will of the entire Pennsylvania electorate. Trump's victory in Pennsylvania was the death knell of Vice President Kamala Harris's candidacy, which hinged almost entirely on a Blue Wall strategy of winning the Keystone State, as well as Wisconsin, which was also called in Trump's favor, and Michigan."

That's music to my ears.

And that sweet song, I'm not hearing it by accident.

I'm hearing it because we put in the work.

I am *always* thinking about registering voters. Believe me when I say it: I love the work that I do. And my mind never shuts off. So even though our formal efforts at EVA focus on the terrain where Republicans congregate—the gun shows, the country music concerts, and the literal congregation—my informal efforts don't have an off switch. In the same way Michael Jordan was thinking about basketball when he wasn't on the court, and Conor McGregor is thinking about fighting when he isn't in the ring, I am always thinking about registering voters. And, at this point, you might say I have a sixth sense.

Here's an example of what I'm talking about: Recently, I was in Lancaster, Pennsylvania at the Green Dragon Farmer's Market. There was an attractive man there, so obviously I wanted to talk to him. But I also had a hunch. When we ended up in conversation, I asked him point blank if he was registered to vote. He said, "No, I've never voted." In my mind, I'm like, "Oh, my gosh. I need to get this man registered to vote. I need to get him registered to vote." In the same way Jordan is daydreaming about hitting three-point shots and McGregor is daydreaming about landing head kicks, I am daydreaming about registering voters.

At this point, I just have a knack for picking people out. And me and this man, we end up talking about parenting, and children, and the future of this country. I'm not even sure if he has kids, but that is the direction our conversation takes. And I'm like, "Sir, I don't know your story, but I do know what is happing to our kids in this country. Their freedoms are in jeopardy. Their health is in jeopardy. And frankly, the way things are going right now they're not going to have much of an economic future." All of a sudden, his wife comes out of the bathroom. She's pregnant, I mean really pregnant. Next thing you know, he's like, "Okay, I'll register to vote." And you know me, I've got voter registration forms on me at all times. I tell him to pull out his driver's license. And we start filling out the form together.

This man's beautiful wife, about to be a mother, she says, "Wow, you're finally registering to vote, baby!"

It was just such a cool moment.

Whatever vibe he had, I was able to pick up on it. And right there in the Green Dragon Farmer's Market, his wife is telling me this is a watershed moment for him, and I learn that he's about to be a dad for the first time. And guess what? He wants this country to work for his kid, for the next generation. I got him to register to vote to make sure that it does work for his kid. I got a plus one in the Commonwealth of Pennsylvania. This man who was a stranger to me this morning, he's now on our side as November approaches. He registered to vote as a Republican.

It's great to get somebody to change their party, but to get a new, untainted, fresh person who has never voted—that high is better than anything I could ever hope to attain from a pill, a drink, or any other kind of vice. It's sweeter than cashing a paycheck, eating a box of chocolates, or inhaling a Wendy's ice cream cone. Whatever your vice is, whatever your pleasure is, it's so much better than that. This is my pleasure. At this point, it's like an addiction. I love that hit of getting a new voter. I want that hit. I crave that hit. I don't need cocaine, alcohol, or the dopaminergic rush of sugar. I don't need to gamble or race a sports car to get that high. I just need to register new voters for the GOP. That's my addiction. And I don't ever plan to give up.

Like the basketball player who will drive to the court in the middle of the night, or the fighter who will throw on his sweats and his hoodie to go on an early morning run—I love the *Rocky* films as much as everyone else in Pennsylvania—I don't have an off switch. I don't have hours when I'm off the clock. And here's the thing, the people feel that energy. That energy is contagious. And it's driving the success of the MAGA movement.

Take Eddie, for example. He lives in a place called Altoona, Pennsylvania, which is in a county called Blair County. Now Altoona is Republican. It's so Republican, they call it Trumptoona. And so, this man Eddie reached out to me with a direct message. He said he's never voted in his life, and he supports Trump. Being that insatiable hyena that I am, I smelled blood. I smelled the fresh meat—the person who has never been to the polls. So I said, and it did take a while for us to figure this out, "I would love to come to your house and register you to vote personally."

Now of course he can register to vote online. He doesn't even have to leave his house. He certainly does not need me to come over. But there's no magic in that. There's no story that he and I will remember. The magic in the work that I do, and that EVA does, is connecting with people like Eddie. It's connecting with them at a personal level. Those connections can't be forged through DMs. They need to be in person. They need to be you and I, face to face, and, as the younger generation says, IRL (in real life).

Eddie will never forget that feeling after a total stranger drove all the way to his house—several hours—just to register him to vote. He's not going to forget that feeling ever. And it's that feeling of being valued that he is going to forever associate with Donald Trump and the Make America Great Again movement. As the poet Maya Angelou said, "I've learned that people will forget what you said, people will forget what you did, but people will never forget how you made them feel."

Here's the great thing about action: When you take action, the karmic web unfolds and serendipitous things happen—many of which you could never have imagined.

When I showed up at Eddie's house, I had the privilege to meet his wife, Billie Joe. I also had the privilege to meet a homeless veteran who they had taken in named Shawn. This American hero was kicked out of his housing. Eddie and Billie Joe took him in. That's the caliber of these people, these people who loved Trump but who weren't voting. When I came in, we all sat down at their kitchen table. They offered me a drink, but I had my coffee. And we're just chatting, filling out the voter registration forms I brought, all three of them are filling out these voter registration forms with my help.

It was a beautiful moment.

But here's the best part: I'm talking to Shawn about the situation that he's in, and how he ended up in it, and I come to find out that something went wrong with the banks, and the banks were saying that he made too much money because he had money in several bank accounts. So he got kicked out of his housing, he got kicked out of his college. He was a veteran going to college, and now he's a homeless man. This man, Shawn, he's got PTSD, and he's got problems with his body from serving America, and they kicked him out on the street.

I asked him, "Who is your representative?" He didn't know. So I pull out my phone right away, and I look up who the representative for Altoona, Pennsylvania is. Who is the member of Congress in District 13? Who represents Shawn? Dr. John J. Joyce came up. Remember, this is Trumptoona. This is a Republican area. They have a Republican member of the House. I tell Shawn, "Dr. Joyce, he's a Republican. He can help you. Have you contacted him?" Shawn tells me that he hasn't. He says it feels like a lost cause.

If I remember right, this was a Saturday. I knew he wasn't in the office. Otherwise, I would have made the call right then and there. I told Shawn, "Monday morning, I want you to make that call to his office. First thing in the morning, you call and tell him your situation." What I did was I posted on social media. I told all my followers that I had just registered a family to vote that has never voted before. I also told them that I met a homeless veteran who was kicked out of his home, and that I instructed him to contact Dr. John J. Joyce's office Monday morning to get help.

When I make a commitment, whether big or small, I honor it. I put Shawn on my calendar for Monday and followed up with him promptly. "When I called," Shawn told me, "they knew exactly who I was. They said, 'You're the veteran with a family that has never voted before, aren't you?' I said, 'Yeah, that's me.'" Now Shawn is in contact with them, and he got a letter saying that they were looking into what happened. Since then, they remedied the bank account problems and they were—if I remember correctly, and this is a situation I'm still following up on—working to get him housing again.

And you know what Shawn said to me? He said, "You're the only person that has ever sat down and actually tried to help me do something. Everybody else told me nothing's going to happen to you. No one's going to help you. It's pointless to try to do anything. It's just a waste of time."

Within a few days of meeting this family who lived in a neighborhood needing some love, and this veteran who everybody else said was out of luck, I was able to get the ball rolling. And in the process, I made another indelible impression on the kinds of people who make our country great. I made another indelible impression for President Trump and the America First movement.

Going forward, do you think this man is going to be casting his vote for a Democrat?

Spoiler alert: I recently did an event in Altoona and invited Eddie and his family. They came, stayed for the entire event, brought their kids, and I learned that they voted this last November—their first votes. What I do isn't so special. It isn't extraordinary, but it is getting lost in our increasingly busy and less personal society. I give my time; I pour myself into people; I invest in them. Anyone can send a voter registration link to a voter, but that's not what I do. Create a personal relationship and show that you truly give a darn. Eddie, if you're reading this, I hope I showed from my actions that I really do care, and it meant the world to me that you came to the event.

To again quote Maya Angelou, "I've learned that people will forget what you said, people will forget what you did, but people will never forget how you made them feel."

That's the difference between sending someone a voter registration link on X and driving hours to show up for them in person.

That's what happens when you take the hard road.

As W. H. Murray has written: "Concerning all acts of initiative (and creation) there is one elementary truth, the ignorance of which kills countless ideas and splendid plans: that the moment one definitely commits oneself, then providence moves too. All sorts of things occur to help one that would not otherwise have occurred. A whole stream of events issues from the decision, raising in one's favour all manner of unforeseen incidents and meetings and material assistance which no man would have dreamed would come his way."

A DM turned into a trip to Altoona. A trip to Altoona to register one voter turned into three registered voters. It also turned into a new chapter in a homeless veteran's life.

That's the power of taking raw action.

That's the power of trusting your gut.

That is the kind of work we do at EVA.

It's gotten to the point where people will reach out to me about their kids. They'll write me a DM that says, "Scott, because of you, I was inspired to run for our school board. I won. We just flipped the school board four Republicans to three Democrats because of you." I love those messages, I really do. I also love the ones I get from parents who write me about their children turning eighteen. These moms and dads, they'll write me a month or even a week or two before their kid's birthday. "Scott, when are you available? My kid, she's turning 18, and I want you to be the one to register her to vote." That—and I'm getting chills writing this—means the world to me. It really does.

I don't want to say your possession, but your child is, they're the most valuable person in your life, they're your world, the most important thing in your world. And if you are going to open up your world, your home, your family, to me, to allow me to register your child at the moment they're becoming an adult, a new voter in our country, that is like the ultimate validation of the work that I do. That's happened countless times, and it never ceases to amaze me. They know they can do it themselves. They know the website URL. They know where to get a voter registration form. But they want me there. This is the magic of politics.

I'm not a pundit. And I don't play one on TV. This terrain that I do my work in is not the terrain of the chattering class. I'm not taking my cues from the professors of political science at the nearby university, many of whom have no experience with actual voters. I'm not taking my cues from abstract political philosophies that have no currency in my day-to-day work. I'm certainly not taking my cues from the polls and the pundits who tells us what all of these polls are supposed to mean.

Remember all those polls that said Hillary Clinton was going to destroy Donald Trump in 2016? Remember all the "political experts" who affirmed that prediction? That prediction turned out to be fiction.

I haven't been polled. Most of the people I know have never been polled. So who exactly is getting polled? Let's it put it this way: if I see the *New York Times* say Kamala Harris is beating Donald Trump by fifty-three to forty-seven points, I know that Donald Trump is winning because that's so close and the *New York Times* is going to overinflate the margins. Moreover, the *Times* is probably polling people who already lean left. I feel the same way when I see CNN flash poll results on the screen. I feel the same about the latest "academic study" that says the Republicans have no chance of flipping Pennsylvania, or Wisconsin, or Arizona.

The majority of Americans, especially Republicans, will be hesitant to tell you how they feel. In fact, many will not tell you how they feel. When they hear a pollster on the other end of a phone call, they hang up the phone. This is the land of liberty. We don't want to be on lists. Especially if we're conservative, we don't want to be turned into data for the next *New York Times* article. So I think polls, especially the ones produced ad nauseum by the liberal professors and journalists—the ones that proclaimed that Hillary Clinton would unequivocally defeat Donald Trump—are vastly under-representative of the way that American voters actually feel. They're vastly under-representative of the way that American voters actually vote.

This is what great strategists like Steve Bannon understand. On the eve of the 2016 election, when the liberal media was trying to take down presidential candidate Donald Trump with its *Access Hollywood* tape, Trump held a meeting in his war room. As Bannon recalls, "Trump went around the room and asked people the percentages he thought of still winning and what the recommendation [was]. And Reince [Priebus] started off and Reince said, 'You have two choices. You either drop out right now, or you lose by the biggest landslide in American political history.' . . . And I told him as he went around, I was the last guy to speak, and I said, 'It's 100%. You have 100% probability of winning.'"

Who was right?

It's that realpolitik that perspicacious men like Steve Bannon are able to grasp.

It's great men like Steven Bannon who I try to emulate when it comes to my own decision-making processes.

Accordingly, I don't let the polls determine what Early Vote Action does.

In many ways, the polls are actually at odds with the work that we do. Excuse my language, but they're a mind F. They're about getting in your head, in the same way Big Brother gets inside Winston's head in *1984*. They're about creating the reality that the liberal media establishment wants. A poll that says Hillary Clinton is destroying Donald Trump isn't so much a reflection of voter sentiment as it is an attempt to shape that sentiment. Here's what I mean: I am only effective when the conservatives I talk to believe that we can win. Otherwise, they're not going to register to vote. They're not going to show up to the polls. The second that conservatives stop believing we can win, we fail. The polls, in more elections than one, have sowed the seeds of hopelessness among Republican voters. Fortunately, not all of those seeds came to fruition.

Ultimately, I need to inspire people. My team needs to inspire people. That's true whether we're in Dallas, Texas, or in cities like San Francisco or Boston, which have long been liberal strongholds. The conservatives in SF voted. The conservatives in Beantown voted. The conservatives in Brooklyn voted. The conservatives in Philadelphia voted. The conservatives in Boulder, Colorado, they voted too. In 2024, every vote counted. Every vote mattered. That's why the Republican Party won the popular vote. This work that I do, that my team does, too, it's part of the reason why Republicans won the popular vote for the first time since George W. Bush defeated John Kerry twenty years ago. The 2024 election wasn't a miracle. It was the result of our hard work.

And, as that story at the Green Dragon Farmer's Market suggests, it's also the result of listening to your gut. I had no idea that man hadn't ever been registered to vote. I had no idea that he leaned conservative. I had no idea that by the end of the day he would be a registered Republican. I'm sure he wasn't expecting his day to turn out like that either. His wife certainly wasn't! But that's the kind of success I have when I listen to my inner voice. That's what happens when you trust your gut, your instincts, and your intuition. In this game, I depend more on that than the latest poll. I depend more on that than what the pundits are saying. And it has panned out really well. He wasn't the only person I registered that day at the farmer's market.

I grew up Catholic, and often I feel like I'm evangelizing. Respectfully, I write that as humbly as possible. I feel like I'm a missionary. While my father served in the Navy, I feel that I'm serving in a very different capacity. I feel like I'm a warrior in a religious crusade to save America from the evil that has gripped it. That's not hyperbole. There is evil in the world. And it has manifested in everything from the sex trafficking across our southern border to the used needles in the streets where children play in Baltimore.

But I'm not selling God. I'm not selling Christianity. I'm not selling religion. I'm selling conservatism and the Grand Old Party. I'm selling liberty, freedom, and the American dream. In many ways, I'm selling hope and change—and not the kind that Obama promised but failed to deliver. That's how I feel every day I wake up. I don't feel like I have a job. I feel like I have a purpose.

That feeling of purpose—and I know my colleagues at EVA share it too—is what drives our work.

It's what gets me out of bed early in the morning, when the sun hasn't yet risen, and the Pennsylvania snow covers my bedroom window.

It's what drives me and my team to continue putting in the work—regardless of the challenges in front of us.

And the more work we continue to put in—day after day, week after week, month after month, and year after year—the results are only going to get better for the Republican Party, the United States of America, and, ultimately, the world. Because when President Trump is leading America, and America is leading the world, it's a world where people are safe, secure, and prosperous. It's a world where everyone, not just Americans, wins.

The terrain of EVA is as diverse as the individuals who make up the Republican party. I've set up booths outside of the Sunday mass at the Catholic church. I've courted conservatives at country music concerts. I've brushed shoulders with them at rodeos. I've been on the streets at Fourth of July parades with my voter registration forms in one hand and an American flag in the other. I've stepped foot inside fraternity houses where students were still partying from the night before. I've talked with the Amish as they sell cheese. I've set up shop at NASCAR races. I've hung out outside of UFC events. If you're thinking of a place that I haven't mentioned, chances are I or a member of my team have been there. I will go anywhere and talk to anyone to earn a vote. My heart is in this and I'm fully committed.

And that commitment has gotten the attention of influential figures who want to Make America Great Again.

I was sitting on the couch at 10:30 at night. I was stuffing my face with chicken alfredo. All of a sudden my phone buzzes and it says Elon Musk is calling. He was calling through the X app. He wasn't calling to talk to me. He was calling to hear me talk to him. When I answered, he greeted me with that distinct South African accent. He said, "Scott, tell me about you. How can I help?"

For a good fifteen minutes, I told him my story, where I come from, how I got involved in politics, and, of course, I ended with the Amish and Pennsylvania. "We must win Pennsylvania, Mr. Musk," I said, "if we want to win the White House." Elon just listened to me as I told him, "We need your finance, sir." "How much?" he asked. "One million would be lifechanging," I told him. He said, "Done."

In hindsight, I probably should have asked for more money; but I didn't. I wanted him to understand that I was serious, that I was competent, that I was not going to be like so many other people—hounding him for an absurd amount of money. I am frugal, money conscious, and practical. I'm not here to waste anyone's money, even if they are the richest person in the world.

Elon Musk was a big reason we were able to hire eighty-seven staff going into the election. Not only did he help us financially, he came out to the Butler, Pennsylvania, rally where I spoke. Elon made an indelible impact with his help. And he helped us win Pennsylvania and, ultimately, the United States of America for Donald Trump.

At the end of the day, this isn't a war of attrition. It's not a war of maneuver either. It's a war of conscription. It's a recruitment war. It's a war where numbers matter. It's a war for our children, and our children's children, and their children's children. It's a war for the heart and soul of the United States of America.

Above all, it's a war that Republicans can—and will—win.

No Time to Waste

At EVA, we are the change that we want to see in the world. Can you imagine if we were proponents of small government, but we had an enormous bureaucracy? Can you imagine if we wanted to abolish government waste, but we ourselves wasted millions of dollars? Can you imagine if we wanted to elect the most inspiring and effective people to our state legislatures, our House, our Senate, our Supreme Court, and our Oval office, but we were hiring ineffective and uninspiring people? Would you take our organization seriously? I know I wouldn't.

EVA is a results-orientated organization. Even when I'm on the phone with my colleagues, I'm on the phone to get things done. I mean, I'm not being mean, but when you call me, I don't want to talk for an hour. I don't even want to talk for half an hour. I love my colleagues. Believe me when I say it, they're great. They truly are. But we're an activist organization. We're not a social club. When I call my colleagues, I get straight to the meat and potatoes. We don't have time for the garnish.

Back in the day, when I was playing chess competitively, I didn't like to ruminate. I wasn't one of those players who just sat there, rapping their knuckles on the table, thinking about their next move. Me, I know what I want. I'm going to make my move quickly. I'm going to make it decisively. I'm going to go for the throat. I'm not here to beat around the bush. Any Republican who thinks we have time to waste, as the Democrats continue to sink our country into the deep abyss, needs to wake up and smell the coffee.

On that note, there's been a lot of hesitancy around voter registration within the Republican Party. I'm not just talking about the leadership. I'm also talking about the rank and file. The millions of people who make this party what it is. Oh my gosh, the amount of times I have heard Republicans express concern, or outright criticism, of what my organization and I are doing—it's really countless. To sound a little cliché, if I had nickel for every time a Republican raised his eyebrows about early voting, I'd be wealthier than Elon Musk.

I kid, but there's a grain of truth in what I said. Still, to this day—after all our success, after that decisive win in Pennsylvania in November of 2024, after I was invited to the White House by the 47th president of the United States—I still see those raised eyebrows. They're usually accompanied by the same questions and comments. "Scott, if we vote early, aren't the Democrats going to know how many votes they need to win?" "Scott, you of all people should know that the voting machines are rigged." "Scott, I'm against drop boxes. They have no place in our elections, and I can't believe you support them!"

Listen: It's not like the Democratic Party has exactly played by the rules. Who knows how many criminal illegal aliens have been able to vote with no identification? Who knows how many Democrats have voted in the mail and again in person? Who knows how many deceased people have cast a vote for Joe Biden and Kamala Harris from the grave? Who knows how many elections have been stolen? Believe me, my fellow Republicans, I share your concerns. And I am in total support of legislation that will make our elections pure again.

That said, if you'll permit me to use another sports metaphor, you have to play the ball where it lands. You can't play the ball where you wish it had landed. If it's possible to vote through the mail, we shouldn't cede that valuable tool to the Democrats. If it's possible to vote early, especially when we might not otherwise be able to make it to the polls, we shouldn't cede that valuable tool to the Democrats. Again, fight fire with a gosh darn flamethrower. We need to vote early and we need to vote often—in every election, no matter what. Why? Because the Democrats are going to vote early. The Democrats are going to vote often. And, unless we meet them head on, they are going to win.

These elections are too important to not take full advantage of every tool that is on the table.

I'm a pragmatist. And there's an enormous pragmatic side to early voting. I can't even count the number of times our beautiful Republican Party has lost a vote not to the Democrats, but to the ether. I'll get a deluge of calls, tweets, and DMs on election day. "Hey Scott! My child just came down with the flu, I'm not going to be able to make it to the polls. Is there another way I can vote?" "The Persistence! I have to work late, and I'm worried I won't be able to get to my polling location before it closes after work. Is there anything else I can do to make sure my vote counts?" "I'm the breadwinner in my family, Scott, and a work trip just came up on short notice. I have to take it. What can I do about my vote?"

It's so tough. Often, I have to tell voters, "I'm sorry. Early in-person voting is over. It's too late to request a mail-in ballot." I try to be as nice as possible, but these are preventable losses. That's why I work tirelessly to use my platform to inform as many voters as possible, as early as possible, of all their voting options. I'm here for one reason: to elect Republicans and defeat Democrats. If I didn't care, if I didn't want to win, then I wouldn't be doing this work. My ultimate goal is to make life better for the American people.

I empathize with these people. I do. I really do. Life happens. You're in business and a deal is on the table. Your boss wants you to fly you out of town to get it done. That's great. You have to provide for your wife and your children. You should fly out of town to get that deal done. Or maybe you get a call from your mother-in-law the morning of election day. She just slipped on the icy bottom step of her front walk. She's on the ground, and she's in pain. You need to absolutely drop what you're doing and drive her to the hospital! Or maybe your dog takes a bite out of a poisonous houseplant. He's your best friend. And he just passed out on the living room floor in a pile of his own bile. Of course you should put him in his carrier and rush him to the veterinary hospital. It doesn't matter if it's election day. You should do it now!

Life happens.

Many of these unforeseen challenges, they actually affect thousands of people on election day. What happens if a hurricane hits Florida on November 4? Are you going to kayak to the polls instead of saving yourself and your loved ones? Are you going to put on scuba gear when you should be battening down the hatches? What happens if a tornado hits Kansas? You saw what happened to Dorothy in *The Wizard of Oz*. She wasn't in any position to get to the polls! What happens if a blizzard wipes out power in Massachusetts? That did happen one year on October 29, just a few days before November 4. These aren't hypotheticals. They're realities. More to the point, they are realities that Republican voters need to prepare for.

The disasters, they will continue to come.

That's why you need to be ready for them.

The fact that I can empathize with every one of these reasons to not make it out to the polls on election day—and there are countless other valid reasons—does not mean I can magically create a new way for these Americans to make their vote count on election day. These people didn't have a backup plan. They didn't plan for the unexpected obstacles to voting that can emerge, often out of nowhere, in all of our lives. And because of that, we just lost a vote. And another vote. And yet another vote. All of these lost votes, they add up. They shape the outcomes of elections. The Democrats have long known this. That is why they vote early—and they vote often.

So whenever I get that question on election day from a panicked Republican tweeting at me, shooting me a DM, texting me, or calling me on my cellphone, asking me if there's another way they can vote on election day, my answer is always the same: *there is nothing you can do.*

These Republicans, who clearly want to make sure their votes count, and who clearly want to do their part to make our country better, they didn't request mail-in ballots. I wish I could help them; I really do. But I can't. On election day, there's literally nothing I can do. They are down the river without a paddle. They are out of luck. That's the reality of every election day in the United States. It doesn't matter if we're talking about our midterms or the battle for the Oval Office. The Republican Party loses votes every single election because Republicans are unwilling to vote early. That is, they are unwilling to use the same tool that Democrats use to win our elections.

I'll say it again. I'll say it until my throat is hoarse and I'm blue in the face. I'll say it until Nancy Pelosi tells the truth for once—which means I'll say it every day for the rest of my life. *These elections are too important to not vote early*. If we want to take back this country, if we want to make sure our voices are heard, if we want to protect our southern border, if we want to keep American jobs in America, if we want to ensure a promising future for our children, and their children, and their children's children, we have to take full advantage of all the tools that are on the table. We have to take full advantage of these tools so that we can ensure that our voices in every single election matter.

When I talk to my beautiful Republicans, when I'm trying to convince them to vote early, I always remind them that *life happens*. They could be the most Type-A, reliable, and responsible person. They could know their location and what they need for identification better than the back of their hand. They could have an hour blocked off to drive to the polls that are only thirty minutes away because they know there might be traffic. But guess what? *Life happens*. God forbid your mother slips and falls, you're not driving to the polls—you're driving to the hospital. You should be driving to the hospital. There are so many things that are out of our control in life. But voting—and having a say over the direction of your own country—should not be one of them.

By reminding my fellow Republicans that life happens, I'm not trying to win them over with some highfalutin academic theory about political elections. I'm not talking to them from my armchair in front of my fireplace with a glass of scotch in one hand

and a cigar in the other. I'm not trying to become the next John Locke, Thomas Hobbes, or Immanuel Kant. I'm a pragmatist, not a philosopher. And when I talk to my Republicans, I'm always trying to make a very pragmatic point: the point of elections is to win them. To do that, we need our votes—all of our votes—to count. If you're willing to give the Democratic Party an unearned advantage every time there's an election for the Senate, the House, the Oval Office, and every office in between, then you're doing yourself, our party, and this country an enormous disservice.

And you have no right to complain when their policies ruin your neighborhood, your city, your state, and your country.

By voting early, you prevent any unforeseen, unplanned obstacles—and, gosh, there so many—from stopping your ability to participate in our democracy. You lock in your vote. Even if you're staunchly committed to voting in person, you can just use your mail-in ballot as an emergency backup. If you get a mail-in ballot, and let's say nothing happens to you, nothing unforeseen or unplanned for arises in your life, and you're in Pennsylvania, you can still show up to the polls in person. At the polls, you can surrender your mail-in ballot. They'll spoil it. That will still allow you to vote in person. It's better to be in that position, than in the position of someone who doesn't get to vote. Mail-in-voting, as so many Republicans have slowly come to learn, is a win-win situation.

If you are one of these people who will always want to vote in person, I encourage you to think about the mail-in ballot like a spare tire. You keep a spare tire in your trunk. Most of the time you will never need to use it. In fact, you may never need to use it. But that one time you run over a broken bottle on the highway, or you take a turn that has a rusty nail protruding from the ground, you're going to be happy—very happy—that you have that spare tire in your car. It's the same thing for the mail-in ballot. You may not use it. You may never use it. But that one time a loved one gets sick, or your car won't start, or your boss calls you needing you to fly out of town on short notice for the business deal of the century, you will be happy—very happy—you picked one up.

It's not just the unexpected events that prevent people from voting. It's an unfortunate reality that voting in person can be a real time commitment. You've seen the photos of people waiting in line for hours. You know that some people have to travel a great distance to get to their closest poling location. We all know that many people don't even trust the electoral process to begin with. So now we're talking about someone who works a nine to five job, with a thirty minute commute each way, who has to prepare dinner for their children when they get home, and who already believes the election is rigged for the Democrats—this is the person I have to convince to take hours out of their day, which they don't have, to vote in person on election day? I think it makes a lot more sense for this person to drop their vote in their mailbox.

If that's not enough to persuade you, then remember this: in 2024, Georgia was decided by ten thousand votes. Is it possible that ten thousand people didn't vote on election day for Donald Trump because something came up in their lives? Is it possible that they didn't vote simply because they didn't have the time? I don't think that is unreasonable in a state with several million people. In Wisconsin in 2020, President Trump's margin of loss was just twenty thousand people. Is it reasonable to believe that twenty thousand or more people would have voted had they had the opportunity to vote early? Again, I don't think it's unreasonable to believe that. In reality, I think it's quite reasonable to believe that mail-in ballots could have tilted these close and absolutely important states in President Trump's favor.

The case is even clearer in state and local elections. On that note, let's think about Pennsylvania for a second. Here's one of the arguments I make to my fellow Pennsylvania Republicans for early voting. Senator Dave McCormick won our state by fifteen thousand votes. This is a state with 8 million voters and it was decided by fifteen thousand votes. Do you know how many people voted early? Five hundred thousand people. I think it's reasonable to assume that at least fifteen thousand might not have voted on election day had early voting and our mail-in ballot not been offered to them. In Pennsylvania, we're not sitting around soaking in the sun like the liberals in Santa Monica, California. Many of the conservatives who live in Pennsylvania, we have blue-collar jobs with long hours. We're police officers, we're firefighters, we're electricians, we're plumbers, we're teachers, we're crossing guards, we're cashiers, we're waiters, we're dogwalkers. In our state, union workers are working twelve-hour days. That doesn't leave much time in the day for voting.

Is it possible many of these Republicans would not have voted on Tuesday, November 5, had early voting not been available? Of course that is possible. I don't see how that couldn't be possible. I know these people. They are my neighbors. They are my community members. They are the people I fight for every day. They are also busy people. They have full-time jobs. Some of these people, they have more than one job. They also have families to take care of. That is, they have an innumerable number of responsibilities that take precedent over voting. It's impressive how many of these people are even able to make it out to the polls to begin with.

And let's not forgot how absolutely close some of these

confirmation hearings have been. Pete Hegseth, the Secretary of War, almost didn't get confirmed. It was a 50-50 tie after three Republican senators voted against him. JD Vance, in his role as vice president, cast the tie breaking vote. If Senator McCormick hadn't been elected that previous November, we would have lost 50-49. Fifteen thousand votes cast by Republicans the previous fall in Pennsylvania—that's what made the difference in Washington, D.C.

For better and worse, there are real ramifications from voter registration. Dwight D. Eisenhower, one of our great Republican presidents and the Supreme Commander of the Allied Expeditionary Force in Europe during World War II, understood that the future of the United States would not only be secured by the battle abroad, but the battles at home in the voting booths. As he put it in a famous speech, "Our American heritage is threatened as much by our own indifference as it is by the most unscrupulous office seeker or by the most powerful foreign threat. The future of this republic is in the hands of the American voter."

On the back of the greatest presidential term to have yet occurred in American history, President Trump's first term in office, we had an election stolen from us. The 2020 election, that was stolen from the American people. I understand why conservatives are concerned about democracy in America. I understand why Republicans have PTSD when it comes to elections in this country. They're not just going to get over that. They shouldn't just get over that. They're warranted to harbor feelings of distrust. After a stolen election—one stolen from the greatest president in the history of the United States—it's to be expected.

In the end, Joe Biden took the Oval Office. The juggernaut of the Democratic Party had done what it has always done:

undermine democracy. In fact, there's nothing democratic about the Democratic Party. The party that rigged the election for Hillary Clinton against Bernie Sanders is the same party that undemocratically selected Kamala Harris as their nominee when they could no longer get away with lying about Joe Biden's cognitive ability. So, when Republicans say voting doesn't matter, I get it. Their distrust, their anger, and their feelings of hopelessness in the face of a rigged system—I have felt those feelings too.

But look, you can't change the system unless you win by playing within the rules of the system. I'm here to provoke change. I'm here to win. That's the one thing about Hillary Clinton, the one thing with which I agree with her on. She said that you can't change the system without joining it. It's the same reason Bernie Sanders ran as a Democrat, instead of someone trying to start his own third party, a socialist party, in the United States. It's the same reason President Trump ran as a Republican, instead of forming a new America First party. Trump, and Sanders, and Clinton, despite their political differences, understand how the game is played. You don't win the game by abandoning the game. You win the game by taking advantage of every strategic move you can make within the game. I don't think there is a more strategic move than voting early.

First you win the game; then you rewrite the rules of game.

The Department of Government Efficiency. The deregulatory actions launched by the Environmental Protection Agency. Even the defunding of Harvard. Donald Trump and the America First Movement, we won the game in 2024. We won it with 77,302,580 votes. And then we came in and changed the rules of the game. No more government tax breaks for antisemitic universities. No more million-dollar contracts for environmental NGOs. No more using government intelligence agencies to spy on the American people. From executive orders to the Big Beautiful Bill, Donald Trump is using his 2024 electoral victory to change the system from within.

When I was invited to the Oval Office to celebrate the victory with President Trump and Vice President Vance, it wasn't because I had the longest hair in the room (I joke!). It was because my commitment to registering Republican voters and getting them to vote early with mail-in ballots is part of what made the difference between 2020 and 2024. You can't stop the cheaters. But you can win by such a landslide that all their cheating won't make a difference. Every election must be treated as beating the cheat by making it too big to rig. That's what happened in 2024. And it's what I hope will happen in 2026, 2028, and beyond.

Chapter 4

THE GREAT AMERICAN PEOPLE

As I constantly tell my team, as well as the people who invite me out to train them to register voters, *location is everything*.

There's a reason the Democrats are trying to register voters at Black Lives Matter protests, Pride Day events, and Megan Thee Stallion concerts. They know the kinds of people who share their views. They know that many of these people are not registered to vote. Above all, they know where to find them.

If a strategy works—and this one works very well—conservatives need to not only mimic it but emulate it.

That's what we do at Early Vote Action.

We aren't trying to find unregistered voters at a convention for Taylor Swift fans. We aren't trying to find unregistered voters at Drag Queen Story Hour. We aren't interested in the places where it's a million times easier to find a radical socialist than a moderate, much less a conservative.

No, we're targeting the places where we know we'll find our people, the beautiful Republicans who aren't registered to vote.

That's why we drive to gun expos, and country music concerts, and UFC events. That's why we're setting up our tables outside Lowe's and Home Depot. That's why we're talking to priests, pastors, and other members of the church.

We understand our people. And we understand the places where we will find them.

While the Republican Party is the party for all citizens who want to Make America Great Again—from beautiful Black women like Diamond and Silk to country bad boys like Kid Rock—there are three groups that have emerged in recent years that I think are absolutely vital for the Republican Party to focus on now and into the future.

The Amish, young men, and hunters.

I truly believe that the GOP will have a strategic advantage to win countless counties across the country, and ultimately our states and the White House, if we can further mobilize these three groups of Americans.

The Amish, young men, and hunters, while they might appear wildly different at face value, share the values of the GOP and its vision for the future of the United States.

But these three groups often stay home on election day.

Elections, quite literally, are being decided for the Democrats because of their absence at the polls.

If the Republican Party wants to win now and into the future, we need to make it clear that we are the party for these folks.

We need to make it clear that we are the only party that won't leave them behind.

We need to make it crystal clear that we are the only party that can Make America Great Again.

The Amish

One thing people don't always appreciate is the beauty of counties in the United States of America.

For example, in Pennsylvania there are sixty-seven counties. Now, every county, for the most part, has three commissioners: two are from the majority party, and one is from the minority party. In Philadelphia, they have three commissioners. Two are Democrat. One is Republican. That's how it works. You're always going to have at least one Republican commissioner. But the Democrats are always going to caucus together, and we're never going to win the election war in Philadelphia—unless, I don't know, God intervenes.

So what's the moral of the story?

The majority of counties are actually controlled by Republicans, because the majority of counties are rural and red. They're not Philadelphia and Pittsburgh. Therefore, we have political power at the county level to make decisions. Those decisions can have far-reaching ramifications for elections.

If I were the Republican commissioners in Lancaster—home to the Amish—my behind would be putting a drop box in their community. And I'd be making sure every member of the Amish community gets a mail-in ballot that they can then quickly and safely put in that drop box.

Why the Amish?

The Amish lean Right. But many of them are not getting to the polls. Many of them are not using mail-in ballots. They're people who share the GOP's values, but their voices are not being heard.

Can you imagine if every Amish person in Pennsylvania—and the rest of country—voted in every election? We'd see a red wave, one that would certainly make or break more than one election in this country.

According to the Amish Studies program at Elizabethtown College in Elizabethtown, Pennsylvania, the Amish are a real constituency. In 2023, they made up sixty-one settlements. They made up 603 districts. Their population in Pennsylvania is estimated to be 89,765 people. That is about one-third the size of the population of Pittsburgh. The Amish aren't just three or four people you see riding horses on a rural road. From a population standpoint, the Amish are a real demographic force.

They are not only a demographic force in Pennsylvania. They are a demographic force in many states. In Indiana, there are twenty-seven settlements. There are 459 districts. There are 63,645 Amish. In Iowa, there are another 9,930 Amish. In Kentucky, there are 15,450 Amish. In New York, there is an estimated 23,385 Amish. In Michigan, there are 18,445 Amish. In Wisconsin, the Cheese State, there are 24,920 Amish. In the great state of Ohio, home to our vice president, there are 84,065 Amish. In short, there are thousands of Amish across the United States—and many of them have never cast a vote. I'm a numbers guy. I've always been a numbers guy. One number I could never forget is that Joe Biden "won" Pennsylvania by eighty thousand votes. Since the stolen election in PA, I obsessed over how we can make up that difference using voter registration. Then, it clicked. There are ninety thousand Amish in Pennsylvania. If we mobilized and activated their community, the Amish could literally help save western civilization.

The task for the GOP couldn't be clearer: get them to the polls, get them their mail-in ballots, and otherwise give them the tools they need to help us Make America Great Again.

Why mail-in ballots? Did you know that the Amish get married on Tuesdays in November? What happens on Tuesdays in November? Election Day. You literally can't make this up. After harvest, the Amish get married in November when farm work is lighter. So, it makes sense why there isn't a huge amount of Amish voting, in addition to the fact that not every bishop is fond of voting. Remember how I always talk about fighting fire with a gosh darn flamethrower? We devised our own storybook ending for the November 2024 election: Use a tool of the Democrats—mail-in ballots—to empower the Amish to vote.

When the *New York Post* ran a headline on November 5, 2024, announcing "Amish turn out for Pennsylvania vote in 'unprecedented numbers,'" it wasn't an accident. It was because we had been putting in the work in the months leading up to that beautiful election. It's because we had a plan to get these great Pennsylvanians to turn out for President Trump. It's because we chose to fight fire with a gosh darn flamethrower.

What do the Amish value?

The are committed Christians, so like most Republicans they value God. They are a group of people, very much like the members of the MAHA movement, who are resistant to forced vaccinations and other forced health measures. They are a group of people who value life, liberty, and the pursuit of happiness. They are a group of people who value self-reliance and hard work, those traits that are so central to the ethos of our founding fathers.

While the Amish value community, they aren't communists.

While they value the land, they are not environmental socialists.

Good luck finding an Amish person at a Black Lives Matter protest, smashing Starbucks windows during an Antifa march, or pitching a tent in Zuccotti Park with the Occupy Wall Street movement.

How many Amish parents do you think are assigning their kids critical race theory and books that encourage their children to transition? If these Amish parents exist, I have never met them. To be a little cheeky, I think you would be more likely to find an Amish person driving a Lamborghini than an Amish person reading Ibram X. Kendi or Robin DiAngelo to their children.

And let's face it, the Democrats are pushing the Amish toward us. As that same *New York Post* article noted, "The Pennsylvania Department of Agriculture stormed Amos Miller's farm Jan. 4 after reports of illnesses in children linked to raw dairy products purchased there. . . . The Amish community saw the move as an overzealous reach by the government and was planning to vote for GOP presidential candidate Donald Trump, whose party favors less government intervention."

The Democrats are digging their own graves with the Amish.

We need to take advantage of their failures.

When a Republican Congressman called the raid "shameful" and said, "it's a shame that small farmers have been pushed into these situations by overbearing government regulatory agencies and lawmakers captured by corporations and monopolies," he wasn't just telling the truth about big government and its ties to Big Food. He was lending his support to the Amish community.

The Amish PAC, for its part, ran a billboard in 2016. It was clear who their "VOTE TRUMP" billboard targeted, as there was a picture of an Amish buggy. What did that big, beautiful billboard say to the Amish? "Hard Working, Pro-Life, Family Dedicated . . . Just Like YOU." That's the kind of messaging we need more of on the Right. That's the kind of messaging that will continue to help the Amish realize that there is only one party who will preserve their way of life.

More Republican politicians, pundits, and strategists need to join our fight to win over this valuable constituency.

This is the message that I brought to Butler, Pennsylvania, before the 2024 election—and, boy, what a day that was!

The Trump family has truly changed my life.

It was President Trump who inspired me to begin cleaning up America's cities and it was his daughter-in-law who had my back when very few would give me a chance. Days after Lara Trump became the RNC Co-Chair in 2024, I saw that I was trending on X. Benny Johnson, a good friend, had Lara Trump on her show and she said that she would like to hire me. Instantly, the video was splashed all across social media and Republicans were buzzing with excitement.

That day, I got a call from Lara Trump: "Scott, how are you doing?"

"Well, I'm trending on social media right now because of your interview."

Lara then invited me to meet at the RNC headquarters in Washington, D.C. This was a first. No one else had ever given me the opportunity. When we met, I explained my strategy to register the Amish, truckers, hunters, fraternity brothers, and push an all-of-the-above approach to voting, as I had done for the last year on social media. We took a picture with the RNC in the background—it went viral. That moment was pivotal: it was a signal that change was coming to the Republican Party and that the grassroots were finally being embraced. I was being embraced.

One thing I also shared was that 13 percent of President Trump rally goers are not registered to vote (shocking, I know). There are

Trump supporters that are not registered to vote. So, I made it a mission to be at every single Trump rally in order to register them and make sure they signed up for a mail-in ballot. Yes, I was there on July 13, 2024, in Butler, Pennsylvania. I don't even want to imagine what the world would be like right now if the gunman were successful, but I thank God every single day that He spared President Trump's life—and our lives.

When President Trump returned to Butler on October 5, 2024, I was also there. It was stoic, it was heavy, and it was almost like a revival. After registering voters and sweating my behind off, I finally made my way to the VIP seating area and took a seat behind Laura Ingraham. Everyone was at this rally, including Elon Musk. The world recognized that this was a history-making moment.

Then, I received a phone call:

"Scott, where are you sitting?"

"If you're facing the audience from the front of the stage, I'm on the left side."

"Lara Trump might call you up on stage."

Immediately, I broke out in a silent panic. It was like time stopped and everything was happening around me, but I was unmoving. For ten enormously long minutes, I sat there thinking about what to say. With nearly one hundred thousand supporters watching live and a global audience, I was going to have the world's attention. What was I going to say in a small, but significant amount of time to do the most good and help re-elect President Trump? All that kept running through my head was, "Scott, you're wearing shorts. Your hair isn't done. You're sweating. They're not even shorts—they're short shorts!" Amongst all the inner turmoil, I collected myself, calmed my thoughts, and focused on what I wanted to say.

Eric and Lara Trump appeared on stage, said some remarks, and then it happened:

"But, real quick—before I go—is everyone here registered to vote? Well, it could be that you've heard of someone who's been doing so much voter registration right here in Pennsylvania. His name is Scott Presler and he has done an incredible job. We have flipped Bucks County and Luzerne County from Democrat to Republican in terms of voter registration. And I would like to invite my friend, Scott Presler, to come up and say a few words to you folks."

My heart was racing. The crowd was going wild. People were cheering. I quickly rose up, looked for a pathway to get to the stage—security removed a barricade for me—and made my way to Eric and Lara. As I was approaching the stage, Lara Trump said, "And he wore shorts for us today, so check out his legs. Look at this."

Walking up the steps, I hugged both of them and Lara gestured to the microphone, "Go get them."

If you were to rewatch the video, you'll see how serious I was. Taking deep breaths and even exhaling loudly, I told the world:

"I wish I didn't wear shorts today.

"Mom and Dad, I honor you on the stage today: Captain Robert Presler and my mom, Carol Presler. Pennsylvania, you have the power to change the world. Pennsylvania wins the White House and so, please, I ask you today: please check your voter status; make sure you're an active voter registered at your current address; and please visit vote.pa.gov and register to vote today.

"A message to our union workers: We want your vote. We want to keep jobs here in America.

"To our beautiful Amish here in Lancaster and across the state, we will protect your raw milk, your dairy, your farming, your school choice, your religious freedom, your ability to afford to have ten beautiful children per family. To our hunters, 30 percent of you are not registered to vote. Please, our hunters, support the Second Amendment—register to vote. To our truckers who service us every single day, request a mail-in ballot or vote early. Lock in those votes. To our sorority sisters and fraternity brothers, please, you have the power—if you're going to school here in Pennsylvania—register to vote legally and lawfully here in the Commonwealth of Pennsylvania. I feel this from the top of my head to the tip of my toes. I love our great county. President Trump took a bullet for us. Please use your ballot and have his back on Tuesday, November 5, 2024, and deliver Pennsylvania for Donald J. Trump. Thank you."

It was done. I did it. I poured my heart out to tens of thousands of Pennsylvanians and delivered the message that I had been practicing for the last year. That one blip in time forever changed my life. Lara Trump, you forever changed me and I am so eternally grateful.

This work was truly on my heart. Even at the Great American Outdoor Show at the Farm Complex in Harrisburg, PA, many of the vendors were Amish. Not only did our team register several young Amish to vote, but I was very upfront in speaking to them. Whenever an Amish person walked by—respectfully, they are easy to spot—I would say to them bluntly and earnestly, "I hope you will consider voting this November. Your community can literally save America." I was planting seeds as early as February 2024.

How did I know what issues to focus on? It's because I spent the last year being an active listener. I have to give a huge shoutout to Juanita Byler. She's the chairwoman of the Mifflin County

Republican Party. When I told Juanita about how it was on my heart to reach out to the Amish, she offered her help. Coming from an anabaptist upbringing, and growing up in the county, she had a familiarity with the Amish and Mennonites that I just didn't. In March 2024, we went on a listening tour. The chairwoman took me to sawmills, dairy farms, restaurants, and we spent a significant amount of time listening to the Amish. I learned that even though we are on the Earthly Kingdom, the Amish seek to go to the Heavenly Kingdom; I learned about how they are pacifists and deeply want peace; and how, ultimately, they want to preserve Amish way of life.

In April, Juanita and I returned to visit with the same Amish businessmen we had the month before. With every single visit, we kept referring to this work as seed planting. Planting seeds meant recurring visits; it meant returning to follow up with each relationship we were building. I was a tall, long-haired, boot-wearing Englishman trying to earn the respect of a tight-knit community. Trust takes time. It takes commitment. I was willing to put in the work. The listening tour gave us even more confidence to speak with authority and it made conversations easier. One thing that people don't know about the Amish is that they are very eager to listen and learn. They may not always agree with you, but they will hear you out.

They had heard us. Already, a few of the Amish businessmen were ready to start talking to others in their community about voter registration. Several also gave us tips on who might be willing to speak with us. This listening tour and an earnest appeal worked. During this second visit, when we came back to the dairy farm, an Amish farmer let me milk one of his cows. Yes, I milked a cow by hand on an Amish farm. By the way, I was sitting on the smallest stool known to humanity. It may not sound like a big deal, but it was. I took that invitation, that gesture, as an honor. I take this work seriously and it was an experience I'll never forget. That farmer did take several voter registration forms from us.

Juanita and I became known as "the woman that goes around with the tall guy to speak to the Amish." That is how the Amish community thought of us and we were okay with it. It meant that we were making a difference. It meant that we were making an impact. It meant that our seedlings were starting to sprout.

So what's the point?

The point, as I have argued throughout this book, is to meet people with conservative values where they are—whether that's at a Jason Aldean concert, a gun show, or on an Amish dairy farm—and to convince them to come out and vote for Republican candidates.

Increasingly, Republican leaders are understanding this. And it's infuriating the Democrats. The *Washington Post* has been observing this trend: "In 2016, when more than 6 million Pennsylvanians voted in the presidential election, the state's 20 pivotal electoral votes were decided by a margin of less than 45,000 voters. Pennsylvania is home to more than 75,000 Amish people, and most who are eligible don't vote." For Republican operatives, they reflect, "those two numbers together add up to one major opportunity—to convince the traditionally reluctant Amish to come out to the polls, where their votes might be tremendously influential. Their project, which started in 2016 with billboards and newspaper ads urging Amish people to vote for Donald Trump, goes by the name Amish PAC."

Pennsylvania: that's nineteen Electoral College votes.

Pennsylvania: that's the difference between President Trump and Sleepy Joe Biden.

Pennsylvania: that's the state where the Amish can very well decide the future of the United States of America.

On the Right, the *Economist*, for its part, has focused on the untapped potential of the Amish vote. "The Amish are members of a devoutly religious community with Swiss-German roots who rely on themselves. They do not pay Social Security taxes and lack health insurance. When somebody falls badly ill, the community chips in to pay for care. 'They are the original Tea Party,' says Donald Kraybill of Elizabethtown College in Pennsylvania." Yet, there is a big difference between the Amish and the Tea Party. "Unlike the Tea Party movement, though, the 300,000-strong Amish are almost politically irrelevant. The church does not encourage voting, and only around one in ten eligible Amish voters go to the polls. As an Amish saying goes: 'We don't vote, but we pray Republican.'"

I'm not the first person to focus on the Amish.

George W. Bush and his team understood how important the Amish were to the GOP's success, especially in the great state of Pennsylvania. They campaigned for the Amish, and their campaign paid off.

"This phenomenon, dubbed 'Bush Fever,'" reflects historian Danieli Curci, "saw unprecedented Amish voter turnout. In 2000, 1,342 out of 2,134 registered Amish voters in Lancaster County, Pennsylvania—which has one of the largest Amish communities in the US—cast ballots, achieving a turnout rate of 63%. By 2004, Amish voter registration had increased by 169%, with 21% of eligible adults being registered."

Who led this effort and what did they focus on?

Curci recounts that "this mobilization was spearheaded by Chet Beiler, the son of Amish parents who left the community when he was three. Leveraging his heritage and fluency in Pennsylvania German, a traditional language spoken in many Amish communities, Beiler developed a voter registration strategy targeting the Amish to support Bush's re-election campaign."

When the Amish stay home, it's not just a problem for the Republican Party.

It's a problem for America.

If we're going to continue to win Pennsylvania and other crucial states, as well as the Oval Office like we did in 2024, we need to continue to mobilize the Amish.

They are going to be absolutely crucial to the outcomes of 2026, 2028, and beyond.

The idea that religion and politics don't mix—that idea of not voting but only praying Republican—needs to be treated as an idea of the past.

"Faith without work is dead." That's a huge argument we use when engaging with the Amish community. Basically, we must couple faith with action. In this case, faith with voting.

Back in the day, many religious leaders were hesitant to talk about politics. They felt like politics was a different beast. Their work was spiritual; politics was material.

But then Jerry Falwell Sr. and other religious leaders came around. All of a sudden, we heard Christians lending their support to politicians like Ronald Reagan and Richard Nixon. All of sudden, Christian leaders were on the campaign trail. By the time George W. Bush ran for office, it was assumed where the Christian vote in America was going.

Speaking of which, did you know that *30 percent of Christians are not registered to vote*?

Imagine how different our country would be if people of faith voted with their biblical values.

But the Amish have still remained a relatively untapped community within our great Christian nation. Those of us who care about the future of this country, and keeping it God's country, need to make those Amish voices count in our elections.

That means we need to meet them where they are, in their communities, on their farms, and in the places where they congregate—even if that means milking their cows.

I'll never forget one *aha* moment in Lancaster County. My Early Vote Action team and I were invited to an Amish benefit at a firehall for a member of the community trying to raise money from an accident. The man who invited us sells baked goods at the Green Dragon Farmers Market. When we first spoke, one of my colleagues learned that the Amish man dabbled in Bitcoin. Yes, you read that correctly. He even pulled out his phone, while his wife was showing baked goods to potential customers. We were allowed to have a voter registration table at the benefit. Slowly, but surely, some Amish women came over to check their voter registration status. So, we pulled out our forms and typed in the information for them. One of the women was not registered to vote, despite having voted last year. As she was filling out a new voter registration form, she said, "Oh, I should probably get a mail-in ballot for my husband, too. We are going to three weddings that day. Then, we'll be out on the mountain hunting."

There it was. A convergence of all the worlds. Everything I had been preaching for the last year.

Did you know that the Amish get married on Tuesdays in November?

Did you know that *30 percent of hunters are not registered to vote?*

To others, it was a simple, mundane conversation. To me, it was validation. It was proof of concept. My gut, my instincts, my intuition, and my persistent work led me to this moment in time. It was a scene I'll never forget as long as I live. We were signing up an Amish woman and her husband for a mail-in ballot for the upcoming presidential election to help save our country.

As I have said before, my approach to politics is pragmatic. I care about elections. And I care about winning them. If there is an effective strategy, I don't care if comes from the Republican National Convention or the Democratic National Convention, the Tea Party or Antifa, the Left or the Right. I care about whether or not it helps us win elections.

The fact is that the Left has been effectively mobilizing people of the faith in a way that I want the Right to mobilize the Amish. They've effectively branded themselves as the party for Muslims. They've trying to brand themselves as the party for Jews, notwithstanding the rampant antisemitism in their ranks. And they have even tried to brand themselves as the party for Christians.

From a historical perspective, just think about leftists like Daniel Berrigan, the Jesuit Priest. Along with his brother Philip, they united Christianity and the progressive movement in the 1960s. Eventually, they were both jailed in 1968 for stealing hundreds of military draft records from the Selective Service office in Catonsville, Maryland, and burning them with napalm. The Berrigan brothers, they understood that politics is for power—and that there is great power in the rank and file of the Church.

In the 1960s, left-wing radicals like the Berrigan brothers—and you obviously have to include Reverend Martin Luther King

Jr., the democratic socialist—used their positions as Christian leaders to build a leftist movement grounded in faith. They repeatedly proclaimed that if you care about the teachings of Jesus, or you care about God, or you care about entering the holy gates of Heaven after you leave this world, then you must also care about stopping America's war in Vietnam, ending Jim Crow, overthrowing capitalism, and otherwise realizing a more progressive vision for the future.

As Dr. King once said, "I imagine you already know that I am much more socialistic in my economic theory than capitalistic. . . . [Capitalism] started out with a noble and high motive . . . but like most human systems it fell victim to the very thing it was revolting against. So today capitalism has out-lived its usefulness." As he also said, "the evils of capitalism are as real as the evils of militarism and evils of racism" and "the whole structure of American life must be changed."

As the Christian Left has repeatedly told Americans, "Jesus Christ was a socialist."

If you're a Christian—a true Christian—those are the footsteps that you need to follow.

But you don't have to go all the way back to the 1960s to see how effective the Left has been at bringing Christians into their movement to radically overthrow the whole structure of American life. The influence of the Left's liberation theology movement, which was most widespread in the 1960s, can still be felt today. As the contemporary activist, scholar, and proud Christian Cornel West reflects:

> When I came into intellectual growth, it was both rooted in the church—I've always viewed myself as a revolutionary Christian,

> in the legacy of Martin Luther King and Fannie Lou Hamer—and I worked closely with the Black Panther Party. So I already had a critique of capitalism, and a critique of empire, and a critique of homophobia and patriarchy, because that's what we talked about in the Black Panther headquarters. I was teaching in the Breakfast Program. I was teaching in the prison, Norfolk Prison, where Malcolm X was . . . I had my own understanding of God and Jesus and struggle and revolution.

For West, and many others like him today, the Father, the Son, and the Holy Spirit of revolution are the real Holy Trinity.

Just look at Florida right now. They have something called Faith in Florida and Souls to the Polls. They believe "the best antidote to systemic racial inequities and poverty is to empower the people who are most impacted and equip them for public and social justice leadership." This is Christianity meets DEI.

As Souls to the Polls, Milwaukee puts it: "We know a strong voting bloc is key to pressing state and local leaders on issues like affordable housing, education, economic development, gun violence, and governmental transparency. Together, we are building a bloc of engaged community members in our mission to channel our faith and bring thousands [of] Souls to the Polls."

As an aside to the Republican Party: Please note that Democrats will utilize every single Sunday and every single opportunity they are given to get more ballots in boxes. I remember reading about how Florida counties were given the choice whether or not to extend early in-person voting another day going into November 2024. The extra day happened to be a Sunday. Every single blue county participated, resulting in thousands of more Democratic Souls to the Polls votes, while red counties chose not to extend early voting. For the Democrats, it was Souls to the Polls Sunday. For the Republicans, it was a squandered opportunity. Let's call it Squandered Sunday.

Ultimately, President Trump won Florida. However, it's mistakes like this one—not using every hammer, screwdriver, and pair of pliers in your toolbox—that allow Democrats to win elections. We can learn a lot from the Democrats. I certainly have.

Wisconsin: that's a swing state.

Wisconsin: that's ten Electoral College votes.

Wisconsin: it's where the Left has been mobilizing people of the faith to march from the Church to the polls for Hillary Clinton, Joe Biden, Kamala Harris, and other crooked politicians.

This is the same spirit that has informed the work of Reverend Dr. William J. Barber II in North Carolina. As Reverend Barber puts it, our current system of capitalism is the problem. "The Pope gets it. They [the Vatican] are very clear that poverty occurs not because people are immoral, but because of immoral systems that have been created."

According to Reverend Barber, Pope Francis "made clear the 'magic theories' of market capitalism have failed and the world needs a new type of politics that 'promotes dialogue and solidarity and rejects war at all costs.' He agrees with the poor people of this nation: We need a moral revolution of values."

These progressives, they are the harbingers of a new epoch—one where capitalism will be a system of the past. These progressives, they understand that you have to win elections to realize that vision for the future. After mass, they'll march their congregations to the polls. They're out there making sure that no stone is left unturned, that no crop is left unreaped, and that no one in their church is staying home on election day.

These progressive Christians, they're mobilizing their congregations across the US to vote for radical leftists, including religious bigots and antisemites like Zohran Mamdani.

This is the Christian Left who the Christian Right must not only contend with but outflank to Make America Great Again.

These religious leaders on the Left, they're smart. They're showing up at Black and Latino churches, where folks have historically shared their values. And these religious leaders on the Left, they're not just Christians. They're showing up at mosques, because they know they can continue to present the Republican Party as the party of Islamophobia. They're showing up at Buddhist monasteries and Hindu temples, mobilizing everyone they can to get out and vote.

But you know where they're not showing up?

Amish country.

The Amish—if we're willing to work for them, if we're willing to show up in their communities and talk to them, and if we're willing to get them to the polls via horse and buggy or mail-in ballot—they will be on our side now and into the future. They will be part of the movement to Make America Great Again.

As I've said a million times, it's up to us conservatives to connect with the Christians who share our values, our hopes, our dreams, and our vision for the future of America.

For my conservatives who have electoral power, it's absolutely critical for you to use it.

When elections come down to a thousand votes, Republican leaders and voters must take advantage of every opportunity to win. From the border, to trade, to rampant violent crime in cities across the United States, the stakes are simply too high to consciously play the game with a handicap. This isn't just about elections. It's about the future of this country—and the rest of the world. We need to win that future for the American people.

Republicans need to heed the wisdom of the great philosopher Charlie Sheen: "I'm bi-winning. I win here and I win there."

Republicans need to take advantage of *every* opportunity to win.

For those Christians who have conservative values, but who still say they don't care about politics, or they don't believe politics and religion should ever mix, I encourage them to really think long and hard about what the Left has been doing across the country to mobilize voters in churches, temples, mosques, and other places of religious worship.

Do you want to cede that territory to them?

I also encourage my fellow Christians on the Right to think about what happens to their communities when people like Nancy Pelosi, Chuck Schumer, and Ed Markey take office. I encourage them to think about what happens when even more extreme candidates like Bernie Sanders, Alexandria Ocasio-Cortez, and Ilhan Omar take office. What will happen to cities like NYC if radicals like Zohran Mamdani continue to gain power in this country?

You can't have a Christian nation that is run by socialists who hate the Declaration of Independence, the Constitution, the founding fathers, and those prophetic words that make the United States of America distinct from other countries: *in God we trust.*

After Charlie Kirk's murder, I often find myself wondering, "How do I coexist with people that want me dead?"

The socialists, the antifascists, and the atheists have their own plans for America. And those plans don't include God.

Is this the country you want to live in?

Is this the country you want to raise your children in?

At a moment when the forces of left-wing revolution are gaining momentum in this country, I beseech my fellow Christians on the Right, especially those who believe that religion and politics should never mix, to heed the words of the late pastor Jerry Falwell Sr., a perspicacious man who understood the stakes as well as anyone before or after him.

"The idea that religion and politics don't mix was invented by the devil to keep Christians from running their own country."

Thirty percent of Christians are not registered to vote.

Young Men

I have so many YouTube presentations about voter registration. At face value, voter registration can seem like a painfully dry topic. It's not as sexy as the Miss USA pageant. It's not as entertaining as a presidential debate. So I always try to crack jokes. But sometimes people will think I'm joking even when I'm not. Can you guess the question I'm most frequently asked when I'm holding voter registration training events? Where should I go to register voters? You know what I say? Lowe's. Home Depot. Your neighborhood hardware store. That answer always gets a big laugh. But it's not a joke. These are places where real men—the kind with big beards and even bigger arms—hang out. These are places where you find conservatives who are not registered to vote.

If I think the audience still needs another laugh, I'll ask my beautiful female Republicans: Who shops at these stores? Mechanics. Plumbers. Electricians. Construction workers. Homeowners. These are the places, I tell them, where you can find a husband. The women, they just eat it up. The men, they laugh. But they know it's the truth. If you're a single woman, go to a gun show.

Get a membership to a powerlifting gym, not a fitness center. Hit up a country music concert. Buy tickets to a UFC event. Donald Trump has been hosting them at his casinos, and enthusiastically sitting in the audience, since the early 2000s.

These aren't places where beta males and limp-wristed guys spend their time. These are places where the alpha males—men like Donald Trump, JD Vance, and, dare I say it, Andrew and Tristan Tate—hang out. As it relates back to the political work I do, these are also places where people who have more conservative views can be found. If the gist of voter registration activism is meeting people where they are, these are the places that should be filled with Republican booths.

There's a reason I'm not spending my days at Washington Square Park or at a Madonna concert. I mean, gosh, walking around Manhattan during Pride Month, it felt like I had entered some kind of low testosterone, *Black Mirror* version of America. The men, if you can even call them that—and many of these men would *not* want to be called men—put the soy in soy boys. But when you go to a gun show in the Midwest . . . Lord have mercy, these are men! I'm self-aware. I know I'm a pretty boy with long, flowing hair, but I'm still an alpha.

Men, including young men, love guns. That's a big focus for our movement. GunShowTrader.com will give you the location for every single gun show in all fifty states. The gun shows, they're fun shows. My team and I are at the majority of them. We're building relationships. We're registering voters. Some of the women on my team are even meeting their future husbands.

You don't need a PhD in gender studies from Yale to understand why so many women, including women who are more centrist in their political views, find Republican men more attractive.

I'm very traditional when it comes to relationships, and countless other men and women feel the same. I think women should be women and men should be men. Up until ten years ago, that wasn't a radical idea.

I know I say this as a man with gorgeous long hair (to be fair, Conan the Barbarian and an innumerable number of other alpha males also have beautiful long locks), but I think there's a clear reason why traditional gender roles appeal to so many men and women. Since the dawn of human history, men have always been the resource gatherers, the providers, and the protectors. Regardless of whether they had short hair like Vice President JD Vance, a combover like President Donald Trump, or luscious locks like Scott Presler, their role in society and their families was unambiguous.

For reasons I will never understand, the Left loves ambiguity. It encourages confusion. It thrives on chaos. Is that a man or a woman? Who knows. What are the differences between men and women? Who cares. The University of California, Davis, an institution that is funded by our tax dollars, lists the different pronouns on its website: he, she, they, co, en, ey, xie, yo, ze, and ve. Are these last seven pronouns supposed to mean anything at all?

I feel bad for the young men who go to college at UC Davis. They might have grown up watching *American Pie* or *Project X*, fantasizing about house parties with beautiful women, only to show up and be greeted by a blue-haired, gender ambiguous person named Lars who expects you to call them "xie." If you ask them what in God's name that is supposed to mean, they'll report you to the Office of Diversity, Equity, and Inclusion. Truth be told, I'm thankful in part that I'm not a straight man in today's society. Imagine the anxiety some of them feel in not knowing—when you're going on a date with a woman for the first time—whether or not she has a penis. I'm not joking.

Of course, I'm being a little cheeky. Most college students are sane. They're not making up new pronouns because they have nothing better to do with their lives. But there's enough snowflakes on these campuses pushing a profoundly destructive, and frankly bizarre, liberal cultural agenda that young men are increasingly feeling alienated from the Democratic Party. According to a recent Equimundo survey, "only half of men aged 18-23 agreed with the statement, 'feminism has made America a better place,' lower than the share of men in older age groups (up to the age of 45)."

For the first time in American history, young men are more conservative than older men.

The data doesn't lie. The NBC News Stay Tuned Poll reported that "about 3 in 4 Gen Z men (72%) say transgender women should not be allowed to play female sports." According to a different data set, "more of the youngest men trust online misogynist influencer Andrew Tate (20%) than trust Biden (15%)." The Survey Center on American Life concluded that "young men are more conservative than liberal (31 percent vs. 24 percent, respectively), but a plurality (43 percent) identify as moderate."

It's that plurality of young men who I know my team and I can—and will—win over.

Just as I was welcomed to the Republican Party as a gay man back in 2016, when I came out of the closet with my #GaysForTrump tweet following the Pulse nightclub shooting, the Republicans and I are glad to welcome the jocks, the frat boys, and the alpha males to the party that still believes that there is a gender binary. This is the only party that won't shame them for being men.

While the Left continues to bash the nuclear family, and monogamy, and other pillars of our Christian nation, young men are truly becoming more traditional. On May 10, 2025, *Axios* published an article: "Young Men Are Leading a Religious Resurgence." As the *New York Times* acknowledged: "young men are now more religious than their female peers. They attend services more often and are more likely to identify as religious." When I'm registering voters, and trying to suss out who the conservates are, I look for identifiers. Are they wearing red, white, and blue? Are they wearing a cross? Increasingly, I'm seeing young men wearing the cross.

The philosophical world view that Democrats have been peddling to young men—there is no God, there is no meaning, and faith is for people who can't think for themselves—hasn't landed in the way they hoped. At a moment when everything is permitted on the Left (drugs, nonmonogamy, and so on), and nothing matters, many young men are turning to the Church to find structure and meaning in their lives. They're not interested in open relationships, psychedelic drugs, and the limitless hedonism that the radical Left has promised since the 1960s counterculture. They're interested in building families, serving their communities, and believing in something greater than themselves.

Russell Brand's transformation from a drug addicted, sexually promiscuous playboy into a man of God in recent years is indicative of the broader shift we are seeing among young men in America and around the world. As the Pew Research Center recently reported, "Among young adults without children, men are more likely than women to say they want to be parents someday." Meanwhile, there is a whole new generation of women who are taking great pride in being mothers, after years of seeing motherhood denigrated by the Left. These "trad wives" are Making Motherhood Great Again. And young men are playing the crucial role of the ying to their yang.

To put it simply, the Republican Party is living through an opportune cultural moment to connect with a younger demographic that has long voted for the Left. Just as the Left has depended on and expected the Black vote, it has also depended on and expected the youth vote—including all those votes from young men. The MAGA movement has disrupted that history, and it's given us a new moment—one where the Left is losing the culture war among young men. "Politics," Andrew Breitbart often said, "is downstream from culture." But it's not just culture.

It's also economics.

The Democrats want the federal and state government to function like the liberal mother who is afraid to tell her children "no." This is the governmental version of the excessively protective and controlling helicopter parent. This is the liberal Nanny State. The reality that an adult man in this great United States of America can get a free paycheck, free housing, and free health care from the government—even if they aren't a US citizen—that isn't just an economic crisis. That is a moral crisis. We defeated the evil empire of communism abroad, but it has survived at home.

More than once, Joe Rogan has said, "Hard times create hard men. Hard men create soft times. Soft times create soft men. Soft men create hard times." There is a reason that Joe Rogan has the most watched podcast in the world among young men. There is also a reason that he and President Trump got along so well when the president was a guest on his podcast. The young men in this country—who I have talked to in Pennsylvania, in Virginia, in

Maryland, in Washington, in Florida, in California, and in other states across these beautiful United States of America—are fed up.

According to the Associated Press's VoteCast poll, "fifty-six percent of young men voted for Trump in the 2024 election." Pace the liberal media, this was a diverse coalition. Whereas places like MSNBC will give you the impression that Trump is alienating Latinos with all his talk about the wall, and deportations, and so on, that could not be further from the truth. "Compared with 2020," writes *Business Insider*, "Latino voters, who make up about 12% of the electorate, had an over 25 percentage point swing toward Trump, based on the exit polling. The exit poll found that Latino men drove Trump's gain, as they voted for him over Harris by 10 points."

What about Black men? Were they driven away by Trump's promise to bring law and order back to US cities? According to left-wing media outlet *Al Jazeera* on November 6, 2024, "Trump almost doubles support among Black voters compared with 2020." More recently, in March of 2025, NBC News reported that "Black men who backed Trump approve of his presidency." Scott Galloway, a professor at New York University, concluded that this was "an election disrupted by men who became disenchanted with a system that had stopped working for them." He called it the "T election." "T" stands for testosterone. I'll add that it also stands for Trump.

But it's not just testosterone, which was in short supply in the Biden administration. Another reason that Rogan and Trump got along so well—and you could say the same about Trump and stand-up comedian Theo Von, who has the fourth most popular podcast on Spotify—is that humor is the universal language among men. I would even argue that transgressive humor is the universal language among young men. Young men, as we all know, like to push boundaries. Today, there's an innumerable number of boundaries that have been created by the Democratic Party. You can't say this. You can't say that. If you don't follow their rules, they'll cancel you out of existence. In all seriousness, can anyone imagine Hillary Clinton kicking back, relaxing, and hanging out with Theo Von? Can anyone imagine Kamala Harris making Joe Rogan and his listeners laugh?

According to Rogan, he invited Kamala on his podcast. She could have had access to the biggest platform in the world to talk to young men, a group that is leaving the Democratic Party behind in droves. Did she accept his invitation? Of course not. "I literally gave them an open invitation," explained Rogan, "I said anytime." Instead, her team offered Rogan an opportunity to come to D.C. In contrast to the normal length of a *Joe Rogan Experience* episode, her team offered him forty-five minutes to an hour. They wanted a stenographer in the room. They wanted her staff in the room. Essentially, they wanted to manufacture an artificial episode of *The JRE* to make presidential candidate Kamala Harris look good.

By contrast, "Trump was really easy to book. Like, super easy. We offered one day. He said yes. That was it. There was no 'what are we going to talk about?' 'how long is it going to be?' 'is it going to be edited?' There was nothing. Trump was just in here by himself. For three hours." To date, Joe Rogan's conversation with Donald Trump has 59 million views on YouTube. That is 59 million views even though, according to Rogan, "there's an issue with searching for this episode on YouTube." The podcast is also on Spotify. According to the numbers, this was the podcast of the century.

The Harris team's attempt to manufacture a fake episode of *The Joe Rogan Experience*, versus President Trump's off-the-cuff, unscripted, three-hour conversation with Joe Rogan, alludes to a core value shared by young men, a value that I try to personify in my grassroots political work: *authenticity*. You can hate Donald Trump. You can love Donald Trump, as millions of people do. But, regardless of how you feel about him, you know who he is. Joe Rogan was more than willing to welcome Kamala into his studio because he wanted to find out who the real Kamala was.

It is the same thing you can say about me and my team. You can hate Scott Presler. You can love Scott Presler, as many people do. But there's no ambiguity about where I stand. There's no confusion about my values. If Scott Presler shows up to an event in Los Angeles, or Detroit, or Richmond, Virginia, you're going to get the real Scott Presler. I'm not going to change the way I talk, or what I believe in, or what I'm willing to do just to please you. I care about America and putting Americans first. That's what I care about. That's what my team cares about. That's what President Donald J. Trump cares about.

The thing with politicians like Kamala Harris is it's unclear what they even stand for. They'll shout Black lives matter! Then they'll defund the police officers who are protecting Black lives in places like Chicago and D.C. They'll say they value public health. But then when you look at the lobbying of Big Pharma, the majority of contributions are going to Democratic candidates; indeed, the Democrats received the majority of contributions in 2024, 2022, 2020, and 2018. They'll say they want America to get a fair deal when it comes to global trade, but then they'll say they hate tariffs after President Trump gets them done.

On that last note, White House press secretary Karoline

Levitt, in a press briefing, recently pointed out the hypocrisy. "Democrats have long said that America has been ripped off by countries around the world. They just don't want to admit it now—because it's President Trump who is saying that. In June of 1996, Nancy Pelosi spoke on the House floor. She urged her colleagues at the time to fight against the status quo trade policies that had contributed to America's trade deficit with China."

So when Joe Rogan invited on Kamala Harris, he wasn't trying to attack her—he never attacks his guests. He was genuinely trying to figure out what the possible next president of the United States of America actually stands for.

He wanted the American people, including the innumerable number of young men who listen to his podcast every week, to find out who the real Kamala was before they went to the polls to cast their vote. It's revealing that this was not treated as an opportunity, but a problem for the Harris team. They knew that there is a big difference between a three-hour podcast and a soundbite. They knew that their candidate wasn't going to be able to filibuster her way through three hours with Joe Rogan. They knew that the American people, especially young men, can smell inauthenticity from a mile away.

In 2025, Bill Maher visited the White House. "I didn't go MAGA," reflects Maher, "and to the president's credit, there was no pressure to." To the disappointment of his liberal viewers, who expected him to return with horror stories about his dinner with President Trump, Maher had a great time. "For starters, he laughs, including at himself. It's not fake. Believe me, as a comedian of 40 years, I know a fake laugh when I hear it. I've had so many conversations with prominent people who are much less connected, people who don't look you in the eye, people who didn't really listen because they just want to get to their next thing. None of that with him."

This is the same Bill Maher who once called President Trump "a crazy, stupid criminal." This is the same Bill Maher who once compared President Trump to Kim Jong Un, the Supreme Leader of North Korea. This is the same Bill Maher who used Representative John Lewis's death as fodder to once again criticize the president. "I watched the eulogies last week for John Lewis and was struck by the genuine outpouring from everyone who ever encountered this model of a man, and I thought of Trump and actually felt sad for him, because at his funeral no one will ever talk about him like that." This is the same Bill Maher whose mind was changed after he had dinner with President Trump.

Above all, Bill Maher was left with a strong and lasting impression that there is a tremendous difference between the America First conservatives—he and Trump were joined at dinner by Kid Rock and UFC Chief Executive Officer Dana White—and the Democrats. "I never felt I had to walk on eggshells around him. And, honestly, I voted for Clinton and Obama. But I would never feel comfortable talking to them the way I was able to talk with Donald Trump. I feel it's emblematic of why the Democrats are so unpopular these days." In the most recent election, they were especially unpopular among young men. As Maher himself reflects, "They lost the men vote a lot last time."

As my team and I continue to show up at the fraternity houses, the gun shows, the UFC events, and other places that young American men call home, the Democrats are going to continue to lose the young male vote by even larger margins in 2026, 2028, and beyond.

The results of the 2024 election weren't a one-hit wonder.

They weren't an ephemeral triumph.

They were a reprimand of the way the Democratic Party has treated young men in this country.

Like Trump, I love to laugh. And I'm not afraid to laugh at myself. When I'm speaking to audiences across the country, I'll say things like, if I forget something, "Oh, I'm so sorry. I had a Joe Biden moment." I'll say things like, "If I met Joe Biden, we all know he would absolutely, positively try to sniff my hair." I said that live on Laura Ingraham's show. She couldn't keep a straight face. She burst out laughing.

If I'm in Texas, I crack Texas jokes. If I'm in the great state of Wisconsin, I crack Wisconsin jokes. When I do Florida events, I let everyone know that I was born right there in the Sunshine State. "Here in Florida," I'll tell them, "I know that there is no shortage of things trying to hurt you. You have alligators. You have snakes. You have Debbie Wasserman Schultz. Oops, did I just say 'snake' twice?" The Floridians, they get that joke every time. They know that the only difference between a snake and Schultz is that a snake has a heart.

Even when I'm interacting with liberals, I have fun. For example, I had this guy write to me on Facebook. He's like, "I can't wait for you to get kidnapped and sent to El Salvador or Somalia." He was likening me to criminal illegal aliens who the Trump administration has deported to third countries they're not from. I could have argued with him. I'm not sure that would have gotten me anywhere. Instead, I wrote back, "I would be very popular." I screenshotted our conversation and posted it on X. It went viral. So many people responded with the tears of laughter emoji. Even people that hate you, if you make them laugh—they can't hate you that much.

The America First movement is reshaping our economy, our public health, and every other area of our society in positive ways. From tariffs to NATO, the America First movement is also reshaping the rest of the world to put Americans first. It's truly a historic moment in world history, and I am proud to be a part of it.

But that doesn't mean we're not having fun along the way.

I had this guy that made memes of me for six months throughout the 2024 campaign. Yeah, six months. And the memes, they went viral. Have you ever seen *V for Vendetta* or read the graphic novel? It's about authoritarianism and revolution. This guy, he made me into V, the protagonist of that story. Remember, remember the fifth of November. November 5, 2024. It was fun, it made me laugh out loud, and it went viral.

In another one, I'm dressed up as a moose. I'm courting the 30 percent of hunters who are not registered to vote. I'm out in the woods dressed as a moose. This guy, he just randomly started memeing me. And it was hilarious. He did such a great job. And he was prolific. I mean, seriously, he memed Soctt Presler so many times that I could post a new meme every day for the last forty-five days going into the election.

And people waited for it. They waited for me as V, as the deer, as all these different things. The guy, his name on X is @6hSense, and he doesn't even have any of his stuff public, but he helped me deliver my message in a way with humor. That humor helped galvanize a lot of support for me and, ultimately, for Donald Trump.

Trump himself, he loves to have fun.

Just look at the sheer number of jokes he makes on a daily basis. The man has a great sense of humor. As Vice President JD Vance recalls:

People always ask me what it's like to be Vice President of the United States, and I'll tell you a couple of stories that illustrate that. First of all, I didn't know the president would make me his vice-presidential running mate until literally the morning of the GOP convention. If you walk back in time, you'll remember what happened. The Saturday before the GOP convention, the president, I actually flew down to Florida to meet with the president. And we talked. It was the first time I had ever talked with him explicitly about becoming his running mate. And he said, "You know, I'm not sure what I'm going to do, but it's probably going to be you. So go have fun the next couple of days." How do you have fun the next couple of days when that's what the president tells you? . . . That's the first story.

The second that I'll tell you: We've probably been in the Oval Office for all of ten days. I'm sitting there, and we had a phone call with a foreign leader—I won't mention who. It's a tough call. There was some tough issues that we have to work through with this foreign leader. He asked me to come sit behind him at the Resolute Desk so that if I need to say anything I could speak directly into the speakerphone. It's early in the administration, so there's not a whole lot in the Oval Office yet. And there was this wooden box with a red button sitting on the Resolute Desk.

I think to myself, "That's probably not a button that you want to press," right? We're talking to the foreign leader, and the president looks over at me, puts the foreign leader on mute, and says, "This is not going very well." And he presses the red button. My eyes get really big, and I'm like, "Mr. President, what just happened?" He looks at me and he goes, "Nuclear. Nuclear." Two minutes later, a guy walks in with a Diet Coke. And he looks back at me and he says, "It wasn't nuclear. It's just the Diet Coke button." That's the

> kind of guy, my fellow Republicans, that we have as President of the United States—a guy who can do a good job, but keep a sense of humor.

For all of us political activists on the Right, President Trump is a model for how to talk, act, and lead. President Trump and his cabinet are a fresh reprieve from the grouchy hall monitor liberalism that characterized the Biden-Harris administration and continues to characterize the Democratic Party. Our movement, it is absolutely effective—but it doesn't take itself too seriously. In fact, I would argue that part of the reason we are so successful is because we don't take ourselves too seriously. Sure, President Trump has just reshaped the world economy to work for Americans, and sure he just radically reshaped NATO, but he'll also joke about Hannibal Lecter. Sure, President JD Vance has played an absolutely crucial role in this administration's accomplishments, but he still can't keep a straight face when he's talking to standup comedian Theo Von or telling that Trump red button story.

In fact, when I was in the Roosevelt Room of the White House, which leads to the Oval Office, Vice President Vance turned to me and said, "I love how you troll Kaitlan Collins." To which I replied, "Mr. Vice President, I would love to be in the press briefing room seated directly next to Kaitlan. It would go viral." It's a running joke on social media that Kaitlan looks like me. You'll never look at her or me the same way again. Actually, whenever she goes on CNN, it's like I'm on television. Thank you, Ms. Collins.

Sure, Secretary of War Pete Hegseth is an absolute leader who can lead us against the cartels in South America and the terrorist cells in the Middle East. Sure, he believes the military should always be prepared to operate with maximum lethality. But he too isn't afraid to crack a smile.

Sure, Robert F. Kennedy Jr., our Secretary of Health and Human Services, is waging a war against the forces of Big Pharma and Big Food, arguably the most powerful forces in the swamp. But this is also a man who will leave a bear in Central Park for no other reason than to freak people out and get a laugh.

In the America First movement, we aren't afraid to joke, and we certainly aren't afraid to laugh.

And for that reason, among numerous others, the MAGA movement appeals to millions of young men.

It's the NELK boys. It's Adin Ross. It's all the young male influencers, many of whom have millions of followers, who helped to shift the young male vote away from the Democrats in 2024. These young men, they're helping us to Make America Great Again.

Instead of meeting young men where they are—speaking their language, sharing a few laughs, listening to their concerns, and addressing them with meaningful policy solutions—the Democrats are trying to manufacture an artificial cultural landscape to steal the young male vote back from us in 2026 and 2028, just like they stole the 2020 election. Even worse, they demonize young men. They pick at everything it means to be a man, demoralize them, and then wonder why men are wholly rejecting the Democratic Party.

As reported in the *New York Times*, "six months after the Democratic Party's crushing 2024 defeat, the party's megadonors are being inundated with overtures to spend tens of millions of dollars to develop an army of left-leaning online influencers." According to a business plan shared with the *Times*, instead of winning over men like Joe Rogan, who is really just the personification of millions of American men, the Democrats are trying to build a Manchurian podcaster. This is how they think they'll win the culture war for the male vote.

To be clear, it's not just the cultural issues. There's a real economic component to the retreat of young men from the Democratic Party. Joe Rogan himself hit the nail on the head in a podcast with Patrick Bet-David back in 2023. "No one is going to run against Trump on the Republican side and win because you're not going to get the Trump supporters. They are all in on Trump. The fact that he was the President for four years, and the country was in a great economic situation, and it looked like his policies were actually effective. And that it looked like the unemployment was down. Business was building. Regulations were being relaxed. More things were getting done. If you just look at it on paper, what he did was effective. Everybody thinks there needs to be a wall." As Rogan notes, Trump is giving the American people what they want.

These are the issues that young men—many of whom are confronting the same realities I confronted when I was a college graduate who couldn't get a job—care about. Regardless of their race, they don't care about "fighting whiteness" and "supporting the trans agenda." They care about getting a job, owning a house, starting a family, and living a life well-lived. Unfortunately, because of the disastrous economic policies of Barack Obama, and later Joe Biden, that reality has become unattainable for many young men in this country. Indeed, many of the milestones of a man's life—a college degree, that first mortgage, the birth of your first child—are being missed because they have been living in an economy that hasn't put Americans first.

From jobs to education, to the privileging of criminal illegal aliens over Americans, our young men are being left behind by the Democrats. In his book *Of Boys and Men: Why the Modern Male Is Struggling, Why It Matters, and What to Do About It*, Richard Reeves is clear: "Things are worse than I thought. The gender gap in college degrees awarded is wider today than it was in the early 1970s, but in the opposite direction. The wages of most men are lower today than they were in 1979, while women's wages have risen across the board. One in five fathers are not living with their children. Men account for almost three out of four 'deaths of despair,' either from suicide or an overdose. The problems of boys and men are structural in nature, rather than individual; but are rarely treated as such. The problem *with* men is typically framed as a problem *of* men." This is the world the Democrats have created.

Of note, Reeves isn't a MAGA Republican. He isn't even a conservative. He's a senior fellow at the Brookings Institution. Yet even he can't help but acknowledge how the Democratic Party has treated young men. "The progressive Left dismisses legitimate concerns about boys and men and pathologizes masculinity." Indeed, they have a whole lexicon they use, one that has been popularized by politicians, professors, journalists, and NGOs. "Toxic masculinity," writes Reeves, "is a counterproductive term. Very few boys and men are likely to react well to the idea that there is something toxic inside them that needs to be exorcized. This is especially true given that most of them identify quite strongly with their masculinity." Of course they do!

I'll be honest, the way the Democrats treat young men, it's a thin line between tragedy and farce. On the one hand, their economic policies and their culture war have done irreparable damage. Men are using women's bathrooms and competing against our sisters and daughters in sports. The men who are fighting to protect their sisters and daughters are called bigots by the Democrats. Meanwhile, men are disproportionately dying from opioids. They're disproportionally working the most dangerous jobs. They're disproportionately taking their own lives. They're seeing their jobs get shipped overseas. And they're struggling to make ends meet. Frankly, it's heartbreaking.

Men are in crisis, and there's only one side of the political spectrum that cares.

On the other hand, the way that Democrats treat young men is so absurd that I sometimes can't help but laugh out loud. As I was writing this book, the liberal media manufactured a controversy over an American Eagle advertisement starring Sydney Sweeney. Apparently, it was "sexist" and "racist" to center a beautiful white woman in this ad. The *Atlantic* published an article, in which they wrote, "her figure has become a cultural stand-in for the idea, pushed by conservative commentators, that Americans should be free to love boobs." If it's now "conservative" to love boobs, I don't foresee the Democratic Party ever regaining a foothold with young men.

You actually have to wonder if these leftists are agent provocateurs. After all, you couldn't imagine a worse political strategy than this. Tell young men that there is something pathologically wrong with them if they are competitive. Treat them as a mental health case if they value physical strength. Call them a conservative if they love boobs. When they don't vote for your candidates, accuse them of sexism. In the aftermath of the 2024 election, *The Hill* ran an article titled, "Democrats' Struggles With Men: It's the Misogyny, Stupid." "Rather than acknowledge the central role misogyny played in electing Trump," they conclude, "pundits blame Democrats for not understanding men." According to this narrative, if you're a young man who didn't vote for Kamala Harris, you're not someone who understands your own interests. You're a misogynist, stupid.

I don't know who is really in control of the Democrats' messaging to young men; but, for a conservative like me, it's like a gift from God. You really could not have imagined a less appealing political party if you tried.

Just like they are doing with the Amish, the Democrats are digging their own graves with young men.

The GOP needs to capitalize on this.

They need to capitalize on this in the same way they capitalized on bringing Christians into the Republic Party in the 1980s.

The future of conservatism in the United States is MAGA.

It's our job to make sure that men—all men in this country—know that MAGA is the only side of the political spectrum that will fight for them, and their wives, and their daughters, and their sisters, and their mothers.

I've said it before, and I'll say it again, there has never been a more opportune moment for the Republican Party to further increase its share of the male vote, especially the young male vote.

Men are in crisis.

And as Rahm Emanuel has said, "you never want a serious crisis to go to waste."

So when it comes to voter registration, we need to make sure we're showing up in the places where this enormous voting demographic is spending its time. Donald Trump went on the NELK podcast because that's where young men are. He went on the *This Past Weekend* podcast with Theo Von because that's where young men are. He went on *The Joe Rogan Experience* because that's where young men are.

We're not all famous enough to go on those podcasts.

But there's no reason why we can't show up at the gun shows, and the mixed martial events, and the powerlifting gyms, and the fraternity houses, and the college football stadiums, and other places where we'll find real men, who want to protect our women, and our border, and our flag, and our economy—our beautiful capitalist economy—from the radical Left. We need to show up because, as I know better than anyone else, many of these young men who want to Make America Great Again have never even registered to vote.

You can go back to Genesis. Eve wasn't created to protect Adam. She was created from his rib. He is her protector, her provider. Other religious traditions present men and women in a similar light. Across the world, and across different time periods, this has been the way of men. Men are here to protect and provide for women and children. That's what makes the Democratic Party's war on men even more insidious. It's a war being waged by weak, feckless men who allow creepy "trans women" to step into our daughters' locker rooms. These are men who allow our women to be raped and trafficked by criminal illegal aliens. These are men who, by the criteria that has been passed down around the world since the dawn of history, are not really men at all.

I mean just compare Pete Hegseth and Robert F. Kennedy Jr. to any politician in the Democratic Party, and you'll quickly see how big the chasm is. There's a reason Mamdani's nickname is "Mamscrawny."

It's not just a chasm in how they look (MAHA, baby); it's a chasm in what they value.

Men like Hegseth and Kennedy Jr. aren't going to let our daughters be trafficked across the border or our mothers get pumped full of acetaminophen and other dangerous chemicals while they are pregnant. These are men who truly put women first. They know that America cannot ever be first unless our women are protected. These men, in every sense of the word, are real men.

You know who else was a real man? Charlie Kirk.

When you think about him, and his life, and what he stood for, and what he devoted his heart and soul to defend, it's not hard to understand why the radical Left wanted to take him out. He had a beautiful wife. He had two beautiful children. He was a man of God. He wanted to protect his family and our country from criminal illegal aliens. He wanted to restore patriotism and a sense of duty in this country. Perhaps above all, he didn't need to use a gun to win young people over. His words won them over. The man who murdered him wasn't just a feckless coward. He was the very opposite of a real man. He was the product of the Left.

As Jordan Peterson puts it, "There's been this attempt to identify masculine competence and power, let's say, but mostly competence, with tyranny and that's very, very hard on young men." As Peterson notes, being strong is "the alternative to being weak, and weak is not good. The people who shoot up the high schools, they're weak." According to Peterson, the Left has created a generation of weak men. It's a weak man who showed up at Utah Valley University on September 10, 2025. It's a weak man who took Charlie Kirk's life.

But, as the Turning Point USA founder knew well, there are still many young men in this country who want to become the strong men we need. As Peterson observes, "There's a statement in the New Testament—the meek shall inherit the Earth—but the meek isn't well translated. It means something more like those who have swords and know how to use them but keep them sheathed will inherit the world."

Charle Kirk was one of those men.

These days, when I read the news, it's unclear to me whether I am living in the United States or a dystopian future like the one depicted in *A Clockwork Orange*. Just look at the headlines. You'll be struck by the sheer amount of sexual crimes committed by people who shouldn't even be in this country in the first place. "ICE Agents Arrest 'Barbaric' Illegal Aliens Convicted of Murder, Child Rape, Sexual Assault Over Weekend." "Illegal Alien Convicted of Sex Trafficking Her Own 12-Year-Old Daughter in Wisconsin." "Biden, Mayorkas Used 'Prosecutorial Discretion' to Protect Illegal Alien Caught Dragging Sex Trafficked Woman Back to Captivity." This is the dangerous world the Democratic Party has created. Think about Nisa Mickens, Kayla Cuevas, Kate Steinle, Laken Riley, and Jocelyn Nungaray. We failed to protect them. The Democratic Party cares more about power—allowing criminal illegal aliens to invade our country as future voters—than protecting our daughters.

When you zoom out and look at the data, it's even more horrifying. According to US Immigration and Customs Enforcement, "New York City is home to more than 58,000 illegal migrants who are either convicted felons or are currently facing criminal charges—and there are about 670,000 of them nationwide." Another data set, provided by the Bureau of Justice Statistics, reveals that "non-citizens accounted for 64% of arrests for federal offenses." The insights of the Cato Institute should be common sense at this point: "illegal immigrants," they conclude, are "more likely to commit crimes than ones who came legally." In other words, the criminal illegal alien who rapes, murders, and otherwise puts American women in danger is not an aberration. He is an epidemic.

Let me be clear: Breaking into the country is an illegal act and it does make you a criminal. Washington State Congresswoman Pramila Jayapal recently wrote on X, "Being undocumented is NOT a crime." I believe that ludicrous, asinine, and downright idiotic statements need to be publicly ridiculed. So, I began firing off a string of replies: "Men can give birth." "Women are treated better in the Palestinian Authority than America." "There are lakes in Florida without alligators." "Joe Biden wasn't in cognitive decline &—in fact—was more cognizant than Kamala." "Being vegetarian does NOT mean you don't eat meat." "Committing crimes is not illegal." "The George Floyd riots were fiery, but mostly peaceful." Each of my replies received more likes than her original post. Mission accomplished. I used humor and intellect to completely demolish her lie and earned more support because of it. This is one way we need to better approach politics, especially in the viral age of social media.

You might hate how he said it. But Donald Trump was right. "When Mexico, meaning the Mexican government, sends its people . . . They're sending people that have lots of problems, and they're bringing those problems to us. They're bringing drugs. They're bringing crime. They're rapists." If men are supposed to be the protectors of society, it's hard to imagine anything less manly than President Joe Biden allowing caravans of dangerous criminals into the country where our mothers and daughters are supposed to feel safe.

When I talk to young men, these are their concerns. The

border. Violence against women and children. Decent jobs. Free speech. Authenticity. Most men still believe in the traditional male virtues: strength, honor, and personal responsibility. They want to protect and provide. They don't want a Nanny State. They don't want to worry every time their little sister gets undressed in her middle school locker room or has to take the bus home in a sanctuary city. They don't want to have to worry about crossdressing predators and criminal illegal aliens when they have daughters of their own.

To these young men, my message to you is clear: *Welcome to the Republican Party.*

Hunters

Many Amish people are hunters. Many young men are hunters, too.

But here's the rub: *30 percent of hunters are not registered to vote.*

Like the Amish, many hunters are Christians. They are people who value the land and what it produces for us. They're not hunting for Beyond Meat burgers in the grocery store. They're hunting actual animals.

Moreover, the hunters—they are men. Many of them are young men. But regardless of their age, and above all else, they are real men. And they do what real men do. They're competitive. They're hardened. These men, they're not complaining about microaggressions and the lack of "safe spaces."

They're out in the woods getting rained on, sweating through their camouflage, and chasing down prey through the forests, rivers, hills, and mountains of our beautiful country.

These men—they are real men.

And their way of life is over without the Second Amendment.

I mean, seriously: Is there anyone who cares about the Second Amendment more than hunters? Is there another party in the US that cares more about keeping guns in people's hands than the Republican Party? Is there any party that has been more of a threat to the Second Amendment than the Democratic Party?

Remember when Congressman and Democratic presidential candidate Beto O'Rourke proclaimed, "Hell, yes, we're going to take your AR-15, your AK-47." That's the attitude toward guns that the Democrats want to see in the Oval Office. In the words of US Senator Corey Booker—the vegan senator from New Jersey—"We need to bring the fight to the NRA and corporate gun lobby like it's never seen before."

These upcoming elections, they are going to have real consequences for our hunters.

Yet, the hunters are staying home on election day.

American Hunter, an official journal of the National Rifle Association (NRA), published an article on August 1, 2024, right on the eve of the most important election in American history. According to data that they culled from Vote4America, a whopping 10 million hunters are not registered to vote.

I'll say that again: 10 million hunters are not registered to vote.

Other hunters are registered—but they're not showing up at the polls. They're staying home on election day. They're not making their voices heard at a moment when Democratic voters—the ones who want to take away their guns—are making their voices heard on election day.

Importantly, hunters are not showing up at the polls in absolutely crucial swing states.

According to that August 2024 NRA article, "States with the most sportsmen not yet registered to vote in the upcoming

Presidential election include Pennsylvania, with 515,277 and roughly a half million each in Georgia, Michigan, Missouri, North Carolina, Virginia and Wisconsin. The states with the fewest number of unregistered sportsmen and women are Arizona at 133,000, Nevada with 59,173 and Montana, 52,233."

A *New York Post* article hit the nail on the head: "If Republicans don't address political apathy among their gun-owning base in key swing states, they'll have far fewer voters in their arsenal to score victories this November." Their prediction was right. We did have far fewer voters than we could have had in that 2024 election. And we had far fewer than we could have had again in our 2025 election.

At the end of the day, when we're talking about hunters we're not talking about some fringe population of people. We're talking about a major constituency in the United States. And it's a constituency that shares central tenets of the Republic Party. It's also a constituency whose very way of life—gun ownership and the freedom to hunt—has been, and continues to be, threatened by the Democratic Party.

Pennsylvania State Representative David H. Rowe was inspired to take legislative action in early 2025. "The Sportsmen Voter Registration Act, legislation that will ensure the availability of voter registration applications any time a hunting or fishing license is applied for, was introduced last week by Rep. David H. Rowe . . . Sportsmen—hunters and anglers—are vital to Pennsylvania. They are economic drivers, conservationists, and defenders of the long-standing Pennsylvania traditions of hunting and fishing. Yet, it is estimated that up to 30% of hunters in Pennsylvania are not registered to vote. This is where Rowe saw a need to raise the voice of Pennsylvania sportsmen."

Republican legislators in other states need to follow Representative Howe's lead.

Having talked to many hunters in Pennsylvania and other states, I know that November is hunting season. I know that some of these folks are out in the woods on election day. I know that they have their commitments, to themselves and their families. I know that not every hunter can make it out to the polls on election day.

You're now about three-quarters of the way through my book. Can you guess what I'm going to suggest?

Mail-in-voting.

Our beautiful hunters shouldn't have to choose between catching a buck and casting a ballot.

Early Voting Action is here to help.

Visit our website, get registered, and cast an early ballot in 2026 that tells the Democratic Party: *You are not going to take away our guns.*

Chapter 5

2026, 2028, AND BEYOND

Hindsight Is 2020

As I was working on this book, an editor at Skyhorse Publishing asked me a question, one that I have thought about more than once: What do I see as the biggest challenge for the Republican Party over the next four years? Do I think that there is a candidate on the Left who can command the same following, however misguided as it may have been, that Barack Obama commanded in 2008 and 2012? Frankly, I don't.

Most of these Democratic politicians have as much energy as Joe Biden, as much intelligence as Kamala Harris, and as much integrity as Hillary Clinton. That is to say, they are just as uninspiring, incompetent, and corrupt as their predecessors who have run for office. Joe Biden got a lucky stroke of lighting with a stolen election in 2020. But lightning doesn't strike the same spot twice. As President Trump continues to drain the swamp, the Democrats won't be that lucky again.

If the Democrats continue to run candidates who are as inspiring as a wet paper bag, then what is the biggest challenge that confronts the Republican Party over the next four years? Many people feel it's censorship. Amazon removed a book written by author and documentarian Matt Walsh. It also removed a book written by Ryan T. Anderson, the President of the Ethics and Public Policy Center. What did these books have in common? They were written by conservatives. And, let's face it, Amazon is hardly alone. With the exception of X, the social media giants have censored conservative thinkers. More clandestinely, they have used their algorithms to make sure that conservative content is not seen by users on their platforms. This is a challenge, one that the America First movement has been working hard to overcome. But I don't think it's the biggest challenge we will confront over the next four years.

The biggest challenge that we will confront in 2026, 2028, and beyond is this: getting all the Republicans to vote in every single election.

In 2022 we were supposed to have this big, beautiful red wave, right? You know, everyone was saying it was going to be a tsunami. "Scott, we got this." "The election is going to be red." "The Republican tsunami is right on the horizon." It made sense why so many conservatives believed our time was coming. For starters, Vladamir Putin had invaded Ukraine—which never would have happened if President Trump had stayed in power. As we all know, strength is the greatest deterrent to war, and you could not have imagined a less strong administration than the one led by Sleepy Joe Biden. On a macabre note—but I need to write it—had the Democrats never stolen the election, Iryna Zarutska would be alive today. She was the Ukrainian refugee that was stabbed to death by a violent fourteen-time arrested Black male in Charlotte, North Carolina, while peacefully riding a train. The judge who released him? A Democrat. The feckless president who paved the way for Putin to invade Ukraine? A Democrat. Elections have consequences.

Then you had the crisis on the border. On June 2, 2022, the *Guardian* ran a headline, "Up to 15,000 may join largest ever migrant caravan to walk through Mexico to US." That was the *Guardian*, not Fox News. But from the Left to the Right, it was hard not to come across media reporting on the thousands of people who felt like they had an open invitation to illegally enter the United States. With Biden at the helm, who could blame them? And while the Left lauded the dissolution of our borders, the rest of America did not. Poll after poll showed how unpopular Biden's attitude toward our border—and our national security—was. Again, I need to write it: Laken Riley, a Georgia nursing student, would be alive today if Joe Biden never became president. Another stolen daughter permanently separated from her family. Elections have consequences.

On top of that, you had a crumbling economy. Skyrocketing gas prices. Ballooning food prices. Things were especially bad in my state, Pennsylvania. When JD Vance spoke inside a grocery store in the Quaker State in the September before the 2024 election, he was clear: "Eggs, when Kamala Harris took office, were short of $1.50 a dozen. Now a dozen eggs will cost you around $4. Thanks to Kamala Harris's inflationary policies, Pennsylvania actually has seen some of the worst grocery price increases of the entire nation, and again, it's because she cast a deciding vote on the Inflation Explosion Act."

In short, life was tumultuous under the Biden-Harris administration, and we had every reason to believe that Americans would vote the Democrats out of office in 2022.

That's what I heard over and over again.

"We got this, Scott." "It's going to be a red wave." "Don't worry about it." "The Democrats have been digging their own graves." "The American people are fed up." "We're going to see a big, beautiful red rebellion across the United States." "Trust me Scott, this is the year we take back power across the country." "This is the year we Make America Great Again."

November 2022 rolls around.

What happens?

In Maricopa, Arizona, Assistant Attorney General Jennifer Wright demands to know why ballots were allegedly stuffed in black duffle bags. "Maricopa County appears to have failed to adhere to the statutory guidelines in segregating, counting, tabulating, tallying, and transporting the 'Door 3' ballots. In fact, Maricopa County has admitted that. [I]n some voting locations, 'Door 3' non-tabulated ballots were commingled with tabulated ballots at the voting location. Further, we have received a sworn complaint from an election observer indicating that more than 1700 'Door 3' non-tabulated ballots from one voting location were placed in black duffle bags that were intended to be used for tabulated ballots," according to an observer of the balloting process. Even NPR, hardly a beacon for the truth, had to acknowledge that "about 1 in 5 polling locations in Maricopa County, Ariz., were experiencing a technical problem with their ballot tabulator machines in the first hours of Election Day." This wasn't an election in a third world country no one had ever heard of. This was an election in Arizona. Who won that election? Katie Hobbs, a Democrat, won the race for governor with 1,287,890 votes. Kari Lake, a Republican, lost with 1,270,774 votes. It was a 50.3 percent to 49.7 percent defeat. The red wave, which I had heard so much about, had failed to put Mrs. Lake in office.

In Nevada, there's a county called Washoe. That's where Reno is. And a lot of Republicans, you know, we like to be away from the government. We like to be in the mountains, in the woods, away from everything else. It snows on election day in Reno, in Washoe County, a Republican county on election day. Adam Laxalt, the former Nevada Attorney General and a longtime Trump ally, is running for the Senate. Many people on the Right are sure that Laxalt has this election in the bag. The champagne bottles have already been bought. The corks are ready to be popped. What happens? Catherine Cortez Masto, a Democrat, wins the Senate seat with 498,316 votes. Adam Laxalt, a Republican, loses with 490,388 votes. The red wave, which I had heard so much about, had failed to put Mr. Laxalt in office.

You can't definitively say the snowstorm stopped eight thousand people from voting. But you can say it made the roads a mess. You can say that people who decided to vote had to wait in long lines. And you can say, most certainly, that some people in this Republican county understandably stayed home that day. "I know I should have voted earlier, and people told me it was a lot easier to vote earlier," one Nevadan admitted to the local news. In November 2022, there were 565,121 Republicans registered to vote in the great state of Nevada. Who knows how the election would have turned out had the storm never hit—or had more of these Republicans voted early. Eight thousand votes. That election was so winnable.

It was especially winnable because it took place in Nevada, a state with ballot harvesting—not ballot chasing. What's the difference?

Ballot harvesting is when you literally collect somebody else's ballot. You can do this in states like Michigan, Wisconsin, Ohio, and Nevada without legal consequences. Ballot harvesting in these states, it's actually been made legal.

Whereas ballot chasing is something a little bit different. If I'm chasing ballots, I can walk up your driveway after I notice your big, beautiful Make America Great Again sign from the street. I can step onto your front porch. I can knock on your door. And I can start a conversation with you. Here's an example of what that conversation looks like:

"Hi sir, did you receive your ballot for this upcoming election?"

"Yeah, I did receive it."

"Okay, well, have you voted yet?"

"No, I haven't voted yet. I'm not even sure I'm going to vote."

"Listen, sir, this last election came down to 100 votes. You can be a hero in this election. You can be the deciding factor of why we elect a MAGA conservative to office."

"I know, but I'm not sure I have the time to vote. I'm really busy. I need to pick my son up from school in an hour, and I still have to finish cleaning the garage before my wife gets home."

"I totally get it! But how about this? Why don't you go in your house, fill out your ballot for whoever you want, and then I'll walk to the street corner with you so you can mail it. I guarantee the whole thing won't take more than ten minutes."

Even though I'll often give them a handout for the candidate I'm supporting, I try to make the whole interaction as noninvasive and non-time-consuming as possible. But, at the end of the day, I want his vote. And I want to make sure his vote counts. So if he agrees to go fill out his ballot, I'll make sure he has the right envelope. For example, in Pennsylvania, you have your ballot, and then that ballot goes into a yellow envelope, and then that yellow envelope goes into a white outer envelope, and then you have to sign it, and then you have to write the date that you are voting. All of those things have to be done in order for the ballot to be accepted.

People can make a mistake. I'm there to make sure they don't.

So when this man is done, I'll be like, "Okay, you know, may I just take a quick look, just to make sure that you've signed it, that it's done correctly?" Yada, yada, yada. And then, that final step, I'll be like, "Why don't you walk with me to the mailbox? It's just a few houses down on the street corner." In all honesty, there are some conservatives who are distrustful of the postal service. "What if my vote gets lost in the mail?" "What if a mail carrier trashes my ballot?" In those cases, I will literally drive that person to an official drop box. So I'm involved in the process. From that first door knock to the moment that envelope is placed into the mailbox, I'm involved. But I'm involved in a hands-off way. *I'm not touching his ballot.*

That's the difference between ballot chasing and ballot harvesting.

Ballot harvesting is essentially that whole process, but I can carry my own little drop box with me. You can do this in states like California, Oregon, and Washington. (Notice anything in common among states that allow for ballot harvesting? Hint: They are all completely controlled by Democrats.) It can be Scott Presler's Ballot Box. And I can go around filling it with votes. I could turn it in right away. Or I could wait until election day, and I can bring my little lock box of ballots, or I can bring a whole big bag of ballots, and I can just turn them all in at once. That's ballot harvesting. That's what's happening in our country.

Of course, there's nuances. The law is not the same everywhere. But it always surprises me how many people don't understand the laws in their own states. So in New Jersey, if you asked a regular person, they'd probably say ballot harvesting is not legal. No, it is. Every person can ballot harvest for up to three voters in New Jersey based on your precinct. So if I have three people in my neighborhood, I can go knock on their doors and ballot harvest. If we're a group of three people, we can ballot harvest nine of our neighbors. If we're a group of ten ballot harvesters, we can harvest thirty people in our community. That's how it works. And those harvests, they add up.

This my point: If we become better organizers, and if we become more educated on all of these different tools, and in what jurisdictions they are applicable, and if we pursue every legal pathway available to us to Make America Great Again, gosh, we're going to start winning a whole bunch more elections. If there's one thing to trust me on, it's that.

On that note, let's go back to Nevada. That state where ballot harvesting is legal, and I can touch your ballot. If I'm campaigning in Nevada, I'm going to touch your ballot. If you're a Nevadan reading this book, I can show up to your house in 2026 to physically collect your vote. That's how it works in Nevada. I can knock on your door and say, "Have you cast your vote yet?" "Oh you haven't? Why don't you let me take it for you?" I can collect your mail-in or absentee ballot. I can collect your neighbor's mail-in or absentee ballot. I can do this over, and over, and over. Before the COVID lockdown protected ballot harvesting, it was a felony. Now it's the law of the land. And the Democrats have been using it to their advantage in Nevada. They've been using it to their advantage in elections across the United States.

So, again: What would that election have looked like if Republicans had voted early? What would it have looked like if more Republican activists were engaged in door-to-door, get-out-the-vote initiatives? What would it have looked like if we too had engaged in legal ballot harvesting and ballot chasing like our adversaries on the Left? I don't have a crystal ball, but my guess is that the 2022 election in Nevada would have turned out different. It's pretty likely we would have secured the eight thousand votes we needed to win that Senate seat. I feel the same about other state and local elections that have been decided by razor thin margins.

Unfortunately, we once again ceded that territory to the Democratic Party, who were more than happy to harvest and chase ballots from sunrise to sunset. Like farmers harvesting crops in the fall, and hunters chasing down wild prey in the autumn forest, the Democrats understand what they need to do to achieve the outcomes they want every time November rolls around. They understand the rules of the game. Above all, they understand how to win the game.

I'll say it again: We need to fight fire with a gosh darn flamethrower.

James Carville, a veteran Democratic Party strategist, put it this way: "The thing I love about politics and sports is that there is an end goal—winning—and there are indeed winners and losers." As he also said: "Winning *is* everything as long as you're within the law. Every decision needs to be made [based on] 'Will this help me win the election?' . . . Now I would betray my own mother to win an election, because that in itself is politics at its highest form. If you're not willing to do that and the other side is you're going to lose."

While I'm not encouraging any Republican to betray their own mother—we'll leave that for the Democrats—I do think it's important to take Carville's approach to politics seriously. He's been doing politics effectively since he helped Bill Clinton take the Oval Office in 1992. And for him, there is only one criterion Democrats need to focus on when it comes to politics: winning. I trust that Carville, like other Democratic strategists, are doing everything they legally can to get those election wins. And let's face it, many of them are willing to do everything they can illegally do to get those wins. This is the terrain of realpolitik that I confront in every election I'm trying to help the Right win.

For the record, and just so we are all on the same page—no pun intended—I'm not advocating for the legality of ballot harvesting. But as long as it is legal, the Right needs to use it—just as it would use any other legal tool that the Democratic Party uses to their advantage. But I'll be the first to acknowledge there are real problems with ballot harvesting, ones that Republicans have been attuned to for years. As Nevada Policy, a nonprofit organization, explains: "ballot harvesting opens the door to fraud." In their address to the public, they outline three of the biggest problems:

1. The person filling out the ballot may have a difficult time saying no to the person collecting the ballot. Think of a union steward, a political boss or someone who controls the purse strings in the family. This is far different than the idea behind the secret ballot.
2. There is more opportunity for ballot tampering, such as "losing" ballots from individuals who are known to have differing political views or are from areas with a strong leaning to one political side or the other.
3. It can open the door to the practice of "helping" elderly or unsophisticated voters by filling in choices, particularly in

> down-ballot races that they might have left blank on their own.

As they note, "it doesn't take many examples of voter fraud to erode confidence in elections."

But here's the irony: You can't outlaw ballot harvesting, unless you have political power. And you can't have political power until you have enough ballots.

Regardless of how you feel about ballot harvesting, it's legal in states like Nevada. And it makes no sense for Republicans to not use a legal—and highly effective—tool to win elections.

Republicans are known for their realistic understanding of the world, and they're also known as the side of the political spectrum that offers pragmatic solutions—rather than fanciful solutions—to the problems our country confronts. Today, there are few electoral strategies more pragmatic than early voting, mail-in-voting, and ballot harvesting.

Unfortunately, it's the Democrats who know this all too well.

Just think about what happened in Oregon in 2022.

I really like to point out this example because when Republicans think of the West Coast, they think of a part of the country that is lost, or they think of states that are lost. If you say Oregon, Washington, California, whichever Republican you're talking to, they'll say, "Those places are too far gone. We'll never win them back." In 2022 in Oregon, we lost an election for governor by just sixty-seven thousand votes. Sixty-seven thousand votes—that's not a lot.

Now, get this, 120,000 Oregonian registered Republicans did not vote in 2022. Meaning, again, that election was winnable. That election could have been ours for the taking. And we dropped the ball. We could have a Republican governor right now, at this very second, and a lot of state legislative districts as well.

Because, you know, it's not just about the governorship; you also have the State House and the State Senate. In states such as Oregon, California, Washington, Hawaii, and Utah, every voter receives a mail-in ballot, whether or not a person has requested one, meaning 120,000 registered Oregonian Republicans received a ballot—and they didn't fill it out, they didn't walk ten feet to their mailbox.

Because of that, Republican candidate Christine Drazan lost with 850,347 votes. Democratic candidate Tina Kotek won with 917,074 votes. That's a 47 percent to 43.6 percent margin of victory. In the world of politics, that's a razor thin win. But it's still a win. And now the great people of Oregon have to pay the price of Governor Kotek's failed leadership.

Once again, I was left asking myself: Where was the red wave that Republicans assumed was right on the horizon in 2022?

Here's the rub: Red waves don't arise by accident.

You have to fight for them.

You have to fight for every single vote.

In my work, what I have to do every day is inspire hope in conservatives who otherwise feel hopeless—conservatives who might feel like their vote won't make a difference. So why bother?

But as all these elections from 2022 have shown, just a handful of votes can make a difference. My job is to ensure that those votes make it to the election officials. My job is to make sure that the Republican Party continues to Make America Great Again.

To borrow the title of George Santayana's famous 1905 art piece "The Life of Reason," the lesson is clear: "Those who cannot remember the past are condemned to repeat it."

We need to remember what happened in Arizona, Nevada, Oregon, and other states in 2022.

Right now, across the country, we have elections coming up in 2026 that are ours to win.

Elections for House and Senate seats. Gubernatorial elections. Mayoral elections. Schoolboard elections. As the Democrats focus on rolling back the progress made by President Trump's second administration and Republican politicians across the country, these upcoming elections might truly be the most consequential elections in the history of the United States.

With the MAGA movement controlling the Oval Office, the House, and the Senate, the stakes are bigger than ever before.

These elections are simply too big to lose.

This country is too great to lose to the Democrats.

That's why the work that we do is so important.

It's not just about protecting the progress that President Trump and his allies have achieved across the country, it's also about ensuring that even greater success can be achieved across the country.

If I show people, like I just posted on X, that we're 74,000 voters away from flipping Pennsylvania, that gives people hope that those 120,000 conservatives that didn't vote previously, well, maybe they're going to vote in 2026, maybe they'll vote in 2028, and that's how we start turning blue states purple and purple states red.

President Trump made a promise to the American people: We're going to win, we're going to continue to win, and we're going to win so much that people are going to beg us to stop winning.

But President Trump can't win this country back on his own. He needs support from the Senate, the House, the governors, the mayors, and even the mothers and fathers who make up our school boards and other forms of local government. To get the right policies passed, we need the right people in office. To get the right people in office, Republicans need to make sure that every conservative vote matters.

It shouldn't matter if there is a snowstorm and long lines in Nevada or technical problems with ballot tabulator machines in Arizona. The Republican party needs to be prepared to make sure every conservative vote matters.

That's why I founded Early Vote Action in January 2023.

Because I said to myself, if we continue to vote on just a single day, we're going to continue to lose. Joe Biden will be reelected. Democrats across the country will continue to be elected and reelected. And the American people—the people who make this country the greatest country on planet earth—will continue to suffer.

Years later, after EVA has proven its success, after I have been invited to the White House to celebrate the 2024 victory with President Donald J. Trump and Vice President JD Vance, and after Republicans across the country have come on board to our movement, I still face criticism from my right. There are still Republicans who are vehemently opposed to early voting. These are people I am trying to win over every day—in person, on X, and wherever else I face resistance.

I encourage them to think about it like this: Virginia, by way of an example, has forty-five days of early voting. Not four days. Not five days. Forty-five days to impact an election. If we don't take advantage of that, and we remain committed to voting on just one day, we're willfully giving the Democrats a forty-five-day advantage.

I'll be honest, that's absolutely preposterous.

We should be giving the Democratic Party zero advantages.

Why would any Republican allow our opponents to have forty-five days ahead of them?

Here's another truth: Those forty-five days save the Democratic Party money when it comes to getting votes. They save money on text messages. They save money on mailers. They save money on door knockers. They understand the rules of the game. And, as 2022 showed us, they understand how to win the game.

If I know that a four-out-of-four person—meaning a person that votes four years out of four years—is going to vote in the upcoming election, why am I going to waste my money on getting out their vote when I should be focusing my money on low propensity voters? These are the voters that need a push: those 120,000 registered Republicans in Oregon who didn't vote, those 75,000 registered Republicans in Nevada who didn't vote. They are the ones who determine elections, for better or worse.

That's where the GOP's money needs to go.

That's where EVA's money goes.

When a presidential election comes down to a hundred thousand votes, as it did in Georgia in 2024, and all the other tight races that I have talked about throughout this book, well, early voting can be the deciding factor between a Republican president, or a Republican governor, and Democrats winning every single swing state.

When I'm talking to Republicans who are resistant to voting early, that's what I emphasize. You can make a moral argument against voting early and even the need to outlaw it. But as long as it's legal, you can't argue with the numbers. The numbers, as the Democratic Party strategists know, are what is keeping them in power—for now.

Furthermore, you can't argue with life. Winter storms come out of nowhere. Cars don't start. Your mother gets sick. Polling machines malfunction. Life, it happens. It's the Democrats who understand this better than the Republicans. And it's a major reason they have been winning our elections.

That's why I formed EVA in January 2023.

To put it bluntly: if we only vote on one day, we're going to lose.

Voter ID Laws

George Jean Nathan, the co-founder of the *American Spectator*, put it this way: "bad officials are elected by good citizens who do not vote."

We need to make sure that every future election in the United States has a historically unprecedented turnout from Republican voters.

In 2026, 2028, and beyond—every election needs to surpass the previous one in terms of voter turnout from the Right.

That's not just how we Make America Great Again. It's how we keep America great.

The forces of the Left are well-funded, well-organized, and ready to seize the 2026 midterms. If we care about the future of this great republic, we need to ensure that doesn't happen. We need to ensure that the polls, from California to Massachusetts and every state in between, belong to the GOP's base.

After 2020, the biggest challenge in 2024 was making conservatives believe that we could win. We rose to the occasion. We met that challenge head on. And we showed the Republican National Committee that this challenge could be overcome. The biggest challenge that we confront right now is getting conservatives to vote in every election, which is why early voting and mail-in voting are so important. From the bottom of my heart, I truly believe they are the most important tools that we can use to win elections.

Why do I say that? Because I know the voter registration data like the back of my hand. Back in May of 2025, we had a primary in Pennsylvania. I was on the ground registering voters, getting my fellow conservatives to take home mail-in ballots, and getting them to vote early—to make sure their votes counted in this very important election. But the Democratic Party juggernaut beat us. The Democrats outvoted us by 200,000 votes. The Democrats, they requested 230,000 more mail-in ballots than Republicans. The Democrats in that election, they knew how to win. They understood the power of mail-in ballots.

Had that primary been on November 4, 2025, which is election day in Pennsylvania, we would have lost everything. We would have lost the Superior Court, the Commonwealth Court, the city council, and the school board. We would have lost it all. The Democrats had a 21 percent turnout. The Republicans had a 17.9 percent turnout. That is unacceptable. It's not how we're going to win Pennsylvania. It's not how we're going to win the United States of America. I can factually tell you right now, unless Republicans get on board with early voting and mail-in voting, we're going to lose in 2026, in 2028, and beyond.

That's what history tells us.

Let's go back even further to 2021. I'm working in New Jersey. I'm registering voters on the Jersey Shore, on college campuses, and in the streets of downtown. New Jersey, the beautiful Garden State, was decided by eighty-four thousand votes. Eighty-four thousand. That number alone is the number of people who stayed home in Bergen County. That important election could have been decided by one county. That election wasn't just a problem of New Jerseyites voting for Democrats. It was a problem of New Jerseyites, many of whom are Republicans, not voting at all.

To say it again, I don't think the biggest challenge that we confront is the Democratic Party. To be frank, the Democratic Party is imploding on its own. Just ask them if they think men should be able to compete in women's sports. These Democratic politicians, they'll shoot themselves in the foot every time. And the people recognize that. Moreover, I don't even think the biggest challenge is the liberal media, and its control of platforms as different as Facebook, the *New York Times*, and MSNBC. To be sure, that is a challenge. But it's really not the biggest challenge we confront.

The biggest challenge that we confront is getting our beautiful Republicans to vote.

That's why the bills—most notably, the Big Beautiful Bill—are so important. These bills are critical to the continued deportation of criminal illegal aliens. These criminal illegal aliens have helped to elect Democratic politicians, even though they don't have the right to be here, let alone the right to vote in our elections. What Donald Trump and the America First movement are doing is giving electoral power back to American citizens. It's incumbent that we use it.

That said, the Republican base that supported Trump isn't just going to come out and mindlessly pull a red lever with an elephant printed on it. Unlike the mindless zombies who put on Antifa masks and smash windows because their communist leaders tell them to, Republicans are intelligent and independent thinkers. From the Boston Tea Party of 1773 to the Republican Tea Party movement that began in 2007, it is clear that conservatives of all stripes—from revolutionaries to libertarian thinkers and MAGA right-wingers—will only support politicians who protect their right to life, liberty, and the pursuit of happiness.

They are only going to vote if these politicians address their needs.

If the president and Congress do not address their needs, our beautiful conservatives are going to stay home. Securing the southern border. Establishing peace in the Middle East. Making America Healthy Again. President Trump and many Republican politicians have proven that they have the acumen and the determination to pass legislation that puts the American people first. They must continue to do that to inspire Republicans to vote for them in 2026. If the president and Congress don't address their needs, we're in for trouble. If the Democrats take the House in 2026, America will be in deep, deep trouble.

Believe me, the next couple of years are going to radically shape the United States—for better or worse.

As of the time I am working on this book, the House has passed the Safeguard American Voter Eligibility (SAVE) Act. It's a landmark—truly landmark—piece of legislation. As the bill explains, it would "amend the National Voter Registration Act of 1993 to require proof of United States citizenship to register an individual to vote in elections for Federal office, and for other purposes." President Donald Trump promised election reform, and the House has moved to make his promise to the American people a reality.

However, anyone that studies government knows that we need sixty votes in the Senate in order to stop any filibuster. I think that the Democrats are going to (excuse my language) move hell and highwater in order to make sure that Republicans are not successful in their fight for election security and election integrity. I just don't think there's any way that we're going to get seven votes and all fifty-three members of our Senate right now to caucus together in order to push forth the Save Act.

I'm an optimist, but I'm also a realist.

That's why the GOP needs a Plan B. That's why we need to come in at the state level in 2026.

My team and I, we're working with Representative Carl DeMaio, a member of the California State Assembly, to get voter ID on the ballot in 2026. Carl has a website, ReformCalifornia.org. His statewide grassroots political movement is, in their own words, "dedicated to taking back our state from the far-Left politicians and special interests." My team and I, who are still based in Pennsylvania, are more than happy to help.

We have to collect one million signatures to get it on the ballot. Really, we're aiming for 1.25 million because the Democrats will surely find a way to strike people off the list. This is something many conservatives don't realize. The Democrats, they'll wipe out a voter who didn't spell his name right. Or they'll say this person isn't registered to vote. For allegedly being the party of democracy, they work very hard to ensure that ordinary Americans can't exercise their democratic rights. That's why we always go above and beyond when we're trying to win ballot measures. If we need a million, we'll come to the table with a lot more than a million.

We're working hard with DeMaio and his team to get it done because we know the realities of national politics, we know the forces that are at work in our nation's capital, and we know that it's unlikely for the GOP to get voter ID done at the federal level.

Believe me, Donald Trump is a political mastermind. He has gotten things done that no one believed he could get done. He has secured the border. He has brought back countless manufacturing jobs. He has made international trade work for Americans again. He has compelled NATO to pay its fair share. He has even changed the physical structure of the the White House for the better. His second term in office has surpassed all of our expectations for what we thought would be possible. He is truly Making America Great Again.

But he is only one man. And the swamp in Capitol Hill is mobilized to thwart his every move. The Big Pharma lobby. The Big Food lobby. The list goes on. The forces of opposition are real. They are well-funded. And they have the Democratic Party's politicians and the liberal media establishment in their back pockets. President Trump knows—and my team and I know—that it is absolutely essential for Republicans to be politically active at the state and local levels. That is how we will support his mission to make America First.

If the Democrats win in 2026, if they impeach the president, and if they otherwise thwart the progress we're making, the Make America Great Again movement will be over. The America First agenda will be done. And it's the American people, from the farmers in Idaho to the miners in West Virginia, who will pay the cost. For them, and the future of this country, we must win in 2026.

We can't have a repeat of 2019, and we cannot allow President Trump to become a lame duck for two years. The stakes are simply too high. In fact, they have never been higher.

As I said before, Republicans aren't lemmings. They're not going to just march to the polls because they're told to. We need to give them a reason to come out to the polls, to get those mail-in ballots, and to otherwise secure the future of this great country. They need a reason to vote. What is sexier than election security? If I can tell people, you can get voter ID on the ballot in California—oh, they're going to come out and vote. That's the entire strategy. I want to mobilize. I want to galvanize. I want to excite people to come out to vote for the GOP. I want them to have a reason other than just a candidate who is running for office. Voter ID has proven to be a galvanizing issue on the Right, and we need to use it to our advantage.

Moreover, it's not just a galvanizing issue on the Right.

It's a galvanizing issue across the political spectrum, which makes it a great wedge issue to bring Americans over to the GOP during these critical 2026 midterm elections.

According to a poll conducted by Gallup in 2024, 84 percent of Americans support "requiring all voters to provide photo identification at their voting place in order to vote." Eighty-three percent support "requiring people who are registering to vote for the first time to provide proof of citizenship." Gallup's findings aren't an anomaly. Also in 2024, Pew Research Center conducted a survey of Americans. They found that 81 percent support "requiring all voters to show government-issued photo identification to vote." Even among Democrats and those who lean Democrat, 69 percent still support "requiring all voters to show government-issued photo identification to vote." In other words, many Democrats aren't as crazy as the Democratic politicians and pundits who don't want voter ID Laws.

Indeed, it's hard to even find public opinion data that shows Americans opposing voter ID laws. According to a Monmouth University poll conducted back in 2021, "an overwhelming majority (81%) of respondents also said they support voters being required to show ID in order to vote, including 62% of Democrats, even as critics contend voter ID laws suppress turnout and unfairly discriminate against groups like low-income, elderly and minority voters." Even when you go further back, to 2016, the American populace remains unmoving in its commitment to fair elections. The measure of "requiring all voters to provide photo identification at their voting place in order to vote" was supported by 80 percent of Americans. Even the majority of Democrats, 63 percent, supported the measure.

While the Democratic pundits and politicians keep saying voting ID laws disenfranchise minority voters, the minority voters themselves don't agree. Seventy-seven percent of nonwhites support a photo ID requirement. That's about the same as whites, 81 percent. To suggest that racial and ethnic minorities need to be protected from voter ID laws is to suggest that you have literally no idea what these racial and ethnic minorities want for themselves. When you look at the data that shows that Trump increased his share of the Black vote between 2020 and 2024, the reason for that increase—at a time when the DNC ran a Black candidate—shouldn't be a surprise. He listens to what the American people, including racial and ethnic minorities, want.

In plain English: Those numbers from Gallup, Pew, and Monmouth University are doing the Democratic Party no favors. Why? Because the overwhelming majority of Americans haven't been sipping the DNC Kool-Aid when it comes to voter ID laws. They understand the importance of election security and election integrity. They understand the importance of identification to keep our elections honest.

This is a great issue not just to get conservatives excited to get to the polls; it's also a great wedge issue to win people from the Democratic Party.

For example, the same year Wisconsin voted for a liberal

Supreme Court Justice, they passed voter ID as a constitutional amendment in the state. Let's make sure we're getting all of these Americans who want election reform to the polls in 2026. In 2026 and beyond, voter ID needs to be a major focus of the Grand Old Party.

While the Left and the Right disagree about the extent to which it happens, we all know voting fraud happens. And the system, as it is designed right now, incentivizes it. If you move out of California to Idaho, you have to cancel your voter registration via paper. You have to mail in a California voter registration cancellation form in order to get removed from the ballot. Did you know that the Los Angeles County Request Voter Registration Cancellation form even says under reason, "Non-Citizen." Our elections, especially in states like California, are so broken and rife with fraud. In recent years, the exodus from California has been dramatic—in no small part because of the Democrats' draconian COVID policies. Between 2021 and 2022, more than eight hundred thousand Californians left the state (with most heading to conservative Texas).

How many of those eight hundred thousand people do you think mailed in a voter registration cancellation form or are even aware that the form exists and they are supposed to obtain one? I'm going to say conservatively, maybe fifty thousand—if that. Remember how I told you that every voter in Oregon, Washington, and California receives a mail-in ballot? That happens whether or not he or she has requested one. Conservatively, I'm going to say that hundreds of thousands of people are still receiving mail-in ballots in California.

So, if I am a Democratic strategist, and I'm a ballot harvester, and ballot harvesting is legal in California, is it possible that people could be fraudulently ballot harvesting from those hundreds of thousands of people that moved out between 2021 and 2022? What about the people who moved out in 2023, 2024, and 2025? There are *a lot* of votes at stake right now. And we know that the Democrats are willing to undermine democracy in our elections. If you don't believe me, just ask yourself: How many people voted to make Kamala Harris the Democratic presidential candidate?

In 2024, Republican California Congresswoman Michelle Steel lost by 519 votes.

Republican California Congressman John Duarte lost by 187 votes.

Especially in these tight House and Senate races, it doesn't take much fraudulent ballot harvesting to tip the needle in the DNC's favor. That's why we need voter ID laws. That's why we need to realize the consensus perspective of the majority of Americans, those who want voter ID laws in our republic.

You can get voter ID laws in three ways: You can do it by constitutional amendment, you can do it by statute, or you can do it by veto referendum. What we're doing right now is we're realizing, okay we don't control anything in the Congress, and the gubernatorial and the state legislature—they're out. Okay, the federal government right now isn't passing it either. That's out. What can we do? What is our methodology, legally and lawfully, to get election security and subvert the obstacles that we have in front of us, obstacles planted by the Democrats?

The answer is citizen-initiated petitions, like the one Carl DeMaio initiated in California. Right now, there are twenty-six states that allow for citizen-initiated petitions.

They're mostly on the west coast.

Right now, we're working to tackle this issue. For example, in Oregon you have amazing folks like Ben Edlt and Michaela

Hammerson working to end automatic vote-by-mail. If they're successful, Oregonians would have to request a mail-in ballot; you wouldn't just automatically receive one. As they know, automatic vote-by-mail raises real problems for election integrity.

When Ben initiated the petition on July 25, 2025, it had already gained at least twenty-five thousand signatures before the end of August. "We've been at almost every county fair in the state this summer," Ben told Oregon Public Broadcasting. That's grassroots activism in action. That's what political change is all about. Instead of waiting for change from Congress, Ben, Michaela, and their team are making it happen in their own backyard.

"We don't want to get ahead of the president," Ben said, "but Oregon is where it all started, and we hope that Oregon is where it all ends in 2026."

It's great Americans like Ben who are keeping democracy alive at the state level. From neighborhood gatherings to public fairs, these folks are working hard to make sure that regardless of what happens on Capitol Hill, our elections will not be compromised. It's hardly a radical thought to think that with more election security, the next governor of the Beaver State won't be a member of the Democratic Party.

It's the same for Washington. Right now, Jim Walsh, who represents the 19th district in Washington state, is working on voting ID reform. If he and his team succeed, Washington will require proof of citizenship to register to vote. Walsh, who is also chairman of the Washington State Republican Party (WAGOP), knows how important this issue is. "Nobody takes responsibility for making sure that registered voters are actual citizens and otherwise legal voters," he has said. "You press the Department of

Licensing, and you press the Secretary of State, and they end up pointing fingers at each other."

That's not how elections are supposed to look. That's not what democracy looks like. Chairman Walsh is absolutely right when he reflects, "Washingtonians of all political stripes have been asking the WAGOP to do something about election integrity in our state." Right now, he and the rest of the GOP in the Evergreen State are doing something. As he explains, "For the past 18 months, WAGOP has been developing and implementing a strategy to take effective action. We studied the state's election system to find the most vulnerable parts. Then, we filed lawsuits and drafted legislation. From there, we've redrafted the latest citizen-led initiative."

I'll say it again: this is what democracy looks like.

At the time I was writing this book, late October of 2025, real journalists were reporting on what was happening in the great state of California. "A massive petition drive demanding strict voter ID requirements is sweeping through California—and Gavin Newsom is scrambling. With over 250,000 signatures collected in just two weeks, grassroots activists say the establishment is losing control of the vote-regulation debate. Newsom's law banning local voter ID rules is now at risk, raising questions about who really controls our elections. Are Californians finally standing up to Sacramento?"

Even in Massachusetts, that stronghold of Elizabeth Warren, Ed Markey, and the Democratic Party, we're working on a petition.

All of these petitions, lawsuits, drafting of legislation, and other actions are happening simultaneously. The goal is to use this synergy as the backbone of 2026 legislative reforms across the country. We're dealing with voter ID in California, voter ID in

Washington, the automatic vote-by-mail in Oregon, and similar battles in other states across this great republic. And our efforts are gaining momentum. Just recently in 2024, the citizens of Nevada voted for voter ID. It was the first vote of two rounds. They went for the first round, and it was passed by over 70 percent. And get this: every single county, including Clark County, home to beautiful Las Vegas, where the Democrats have a majority, voted for voter ID. This isn't a partisan issue. This is a fundamental issue of democracy. And the American people know it.

You can't have a republic without fair elections. And you can't have fair elections without election integrity. There's no integrity when people don't even need to show an ID to prove that they are who they say they are. While the Left loves to complain about the death of the public's trust in our longstanding political institutions, they fail to see that they are the gravediggers. They fail to see that they are the ones wielding the shovels. Why should anyone, including members of their own party, trust our elections when it's a known fact that they are not protected?

Election integrity—that's not a radical expectation. Around the world, it's just common sense. The list of countries that require voter ID includes: Iceland, Sweden, New Zealand, Denmark, Ireland, Switzerland, Finland, Australia, Luxembourg, Netherlands, Germany, Austria, Malta, Spain, Uruguay, Japan, Italy, France, South Korea, Costa Rica, and Botswana.

You know who else requires voter ID?

Portugal, Estonia, Israel, Czech Republic, India, Taiwan, Chile, Belgium, Cyprus, Slovenia, Lithuania, South Africa, Jamaica, Latvia, Slovakia, Greece, Panama, Bulgaria, Indonesia, Argentina, Poland, Brazil, Ghana, Croatia, Hungry, Columbia, Peru, El Salvador, Romania, Serbia, Hong Kong, Singapore, Georgia,

Honduras, Ecuador, Bangladesh, Ukraine, Bolivia, Turkey, Kena, Thailand, Nicaragua, Palestine, Pakistan, Iraq, Haiti, and even Nicolás Maduro's Venezuela!

The list just goes on, and on, and on.

From Mauritius to the United Kingdom, voter ID laws are the norm.

Even our neighbors—Canada and Mexico—have voter ID laws.

Why are there so many voter ID laws around the world?

According to the title of a research paper published by Lake Forest college Professor John R. Lott, Jr., the answer is obvious. "Why Do Most Countries Require Photo Voter IDs?: They Have Seen Massive Vote Fraud Problems." Professor Lott understands the data. As he notes, "What can we learn from countries that have experienced significant vote fraud? Far from disenfranchising voters, after Mexico's strict anti-fraud rules were passed, the voter participation rates during the next three presidential elections averaged nine percentage points higher than during the three elections before the change."

When people feel that elections are secure, when they believe that people who don't have the legal right to vote won't have the ability to vote, and when they trust the political process—that's when they show up to the polls. That's when they defend our political institutions. That's when they accept election results, even if they are results that they themselves didn't vote for. Electoral integrity is absolutely central to increasing democratic participation, faith in our political process and institutions, and the continued existence of our democracy. There might be no better solution for the level of polarization in this country than elections that everyone believes are fair. There's certainly no better solution for increasing people's willingness to participate in our political process.

I like to break things down in the simplest way possible, so here's another way to think about it: Let's say you're a kid who wants to participate in a high school wrestling tournament. Ostensibly, you're only supposed to be competing against other high schoolers. But let's say the officials don't actually check the ages of the wrestlers who compete. There's no ID requirement. You just take everyone at their word. Looking around, you see wrestlers who are clearly in their thirties taking to the mat. In fact, it's been revealed that many adults participate in this tournament because the age rules are not enforced. If you're a high schooler, is that going to make you want to compete? No, you're probably going to stay home because the whole tournament looks corrupt, rigged, and virtually pointless to participate in.

As Professor Lott points out, when election rules are enforced with voter ID requirements, it doesn't reduce the number of people going to the polls; it actually increases it. That makes sense. Why would anyone participate in anything that is crooked? You're not going to play a board game with a group of cheaters who don't follow the rules. You're not going to place a sports bet when you know the officials don't enforce the rules. So, when it comes to something significantly more important, it makes absolute sense that turnout is higher when voter ID is both required and enforced.

Yet, the data about the relationship between voter ID and voter turnout has not crushed the liberal narrative in the United States that voter ID requirements decrease voter turnout. Reality hasn't crushed the liberal narrative in the United States, even if it has crushed it in other countries—where voter ID has been and will continue to be the norm. Why is the United States so distinct?

If you want to answer that question, you need to look at the liberal media. As President Trump has said, the liberal press is "truly the enemy of the people."

"The American media keeps telling us two 'facts.' Voter ID laws are 'racist,' and election fraud claims are 'false' and 'baseless' . . . David Leonhardt at the *New York Times* said that he didn't take his comments 'lightly' but labeled state ID and voting laws as showing 'the Republican Party's growing discomfort with democracy.' 'It's dangerously anti-democratic,' another article in the *Times* quotes Kenneth Mayer, a political scientist at the University of Wisconsin," writes Professor Lott. "But by that standard," Lott points out, "all of Europe, indeed, virtually all the developed world, is 'antidemocratic.'"

At this point, it's harder to find a democratized country, or at this point really any country in the world—again, even Nicolás Maduro's Venezuela has voter ID requirements—that doesn't ask voters to show ID.

I'll ask the question again: Why is the United States such an outlier?

The answer is the America Left, which rhymes with theft.

For decades, the Left has been waging a war against voter ID laws.

According to the League of Women Voters, "While supporters argue that voter photo ID laws are necessary to prevent voter fraud and ensure the integrity of elections, reality tells a different story. Not only do these measures disproportionately impact Black, Native, elderly, and student voters, but they also fail to effectively address any real issues related to election integrity—the very thing advocates say these measures are designed to do."

According to the Brennan Center for Justice, "Overly burdensome photo ID requirements block millions of eligible American citizens from voting. As many as 11 percent of eligible voters do not have the kind of ID that is required by states with strict ID requirements, and that percentage is even higher among seniors, minorities, people with disabilities, low-income voters, and students. Many citizens find it difficult to obtain government photo IDs because the necessary documentation, such as a birth certificate, is often difficult or expensive to acquire."

According to the Center for Democracy and Civic Engagement, "As voter ID laws have spread and gained public support, the danger of ID based disenfranchisement—eligible voters being denied their right to vote because they cannot meet or are confused about a state ID requirement—potentially grows . . . there is urgent work to be done to help Americans without any form of ID access the ballot."

It's not just the nonprofits who are fighting hard to combat voter ID laws.

It's lawyers on the Left.

According to the American Civil Liberties Union, "Unnecessarily strict voter identification laws are a part of an ongoing strategy to roll back decades of progress on voting rights . . . Overly burdensome photo ID laws deprive many voters of their right to vote, reduce participation, and stand in direct opposition to our country's trend of including more Americans in the democratic process. Many Americans do not have one of the forms of government-issued photo identification that state laws list as acceptable for voting. These voters are disproportionately low-income, racial and ethnic minorities, the elderly, and people with disabilities."

In short, if you're for voter ID—you must be against low-income, racial and ethnic minorities, the elderly, and people with disabilities. This is how the Left frames the issue. Just look at the headlines:

"How ID Requirements Harm Marginalized Communities and Their Right to Vote."

"How Voter ID Laws Suppress Transgender Voters."

"Voter Identification Laws and the Suppression of Minority Votes."

"Voter ID Rules Are Racist—Let's Get Rid of Them Once and for All."

"Courts Are Finally Pointing Out the Racism Behind Voter ID Laws."

"Are Today's Voter Suppression Laws the New Jim Crow?"

"The SAVE Act Would Disenfranchise Millions of Citizens."

As the *New York Times* writes, there is "no question that a lot of Republican operatives pushing voter ID laws are cynics who expect their party to benefit from lower minority turnout, and a number of professional right-wing partisans—including our president—see an upside in frightening their voters or viewers with the racialized threat of 'urban' ballot-stuffing." As they also note, "the voter ID debate essentially involves Republicans whipping themselves into a panic over a problem that doesn't meaningfully affect their chances of winning elections."

If you disagree, you must want to disenfranchise minorities.

You must be on "the wrong side of history."

Even worse, you must be a nazi.

As reported in *Slate*, Democrat Pat Lehman "invoked Adolf

Hitler to argue that Republicans are lying when they say voter ID efforts are designed to combat voter fraud." What did Lehman, who has been described as the "dean of the Kansas delegation," say? "It's like Hitler said, if you're going to tell a lie, tell a big lie, and if you tell it often enough and say it in a loud enough voice, some people are going to believe you." We've now reached a point where the people asking to see voter IDs are being compared to the people who orchestrated a genocide. While the Democrats won't support our constitutional right to bear arms, they love to escalate the rhetorical arms race.

According to the Left, anyone who wants voters to have to show ID is against Black people, trans people, Native Americans, the elderly, people with disabilities, low-income Americans, and students. They're also against people with "neurodiversity," who apparently are too neurologically diverse to have ID. When it comes to any kind of "marginalization," voter ID is going to make it harder for the "marginalized" to have a voice. This is what everyone from the *NYT* to the nonprofit organizations, to the activists in the streets, and the lefty lawyers in the courts are telling the American people.

I assume it's only going to be a matter of time before the Left is telling me that voter ID disproportionately disenfranchises gay people like me—as if sexuality has anything to do with the fight for more secure elections.

As you've no doubt noticed, especially in recent years, this is how the Left responds to any policy, position, or argument it doesn't like. It associates you with racism, sexism, ableism, homophobia, Islamophobia, and so on. Instead of an argument, the Left is always prepared to offer an ad hominem attack that puts you on the "wrong side of history." After all, wasn't it racists who implemented literary tests to prevent African Americans from voting? You're not on their side, are you? When Elon announced in 2024 that he was going to purchase Twitter, I put out a spicy tweet that I knew liberals could understand: "Democrats haven't been this mad about an African American fighting for free speech since they invented the KKK." It went supernova viral. The truth hurts.

I'll be honest, there's a lot of liberal racism in these conversations about voter ID laws. Just ask the Democrats what they really think, and they'll tell you that Black people, or Native American people, or whoever, don't know how to get IDs. But then you watch videos where people will go meet members of these racial and ethnic communities on the street. They'll go talk to members of the Black community, or the "Latin/x" community, or folks on a reservation, and they'll say, "Hey, do you have an ID?" And they'll pull it out right in front of them.

They'll say, "Hey, do you know where the DMV is?" "Yeah, I know where the DMV is." "Why wouldn't I know where the DMV is? I own a car. I need to know where it is." They'll ask these folks, "Do you carry your license with you everywhere?" And they'll be like, "Yeah, it's in my wallet." There something darkly comical about these street videos. It's almost like the liberal elite has never actually talked to a Black person, or a Native American, or an American who was born in Mexico.

Just watch what happens when these street interviewers go out and ask white people of the liberal persuasion—who are also usually highly educated and more affluent—why are you against voter ID laws? They'll tell you it's because Black people and "Latin/x" people don't have IDs. They'll tell you that they can't afford them, or they can't figure out how to fill out the forms, or they don't have internet, or they don't know how to use the internet, or they have no idea where the DMV is, or they have no way of getting there. For every Democrat who calls Republicans racist for wanting to secure the border, look at how south Texas voted in the 2024 presidential election—border towns are quickly moving to the right. I'm certain that Democrats will soon begin calling Hispanic immigrants racist and xenophobic.

They treat minority voters like ignorant savages on an undiscovered island.

In his book *Woke Antiracism*, John McWhorter, a Columbia University professor and himself an African American, has observed this phenomenon on the Left. "White people calling themselves our saviors make Black people look like the dumbest, weakest, most self-indulgent human beings in the history of our species, and teach Black people to revel in that status and cherish it as making us special." Sociologists call this the "racism of low expectations." In recent years, it has become a staple of the Democratic Party's rhetoric around voter ID laws.

It doesn't even matter that Native Americans, African Americans, Hispanics, and members of other racial and ethnic minority groups have all voted for voter ID laws. The Left still contends that these laws, and the people who vote for them, and especially the party that pushes for them, are racist. When people talk about the GOP as the party of reality, this is what they're getting at. The Left, especially in the age of wokeness, has become unmoored from the very people they purport to represent.

To restate the point, voter ID laws are the norm around the world, even in countries—like Mexico, Peru, and Colombia—that could hardly be classified as "white supremacist." To again quote Professor Lott: "In the US, Georgia's new absentee provisions raised a ruckus despite still being much less restrictive than the rest of the world. Anyone who wants an absentee ballot can obtain one; you don't need a reason, such as being out of town, but you must have an ID to get an absentee ballot. Seventy-four percent of European countries entirely ban absentee voting for citizens who reside domestically. Another 6% limit it to those hospitalized or in the military, and they require third-party verification and a photo voter ID. Another 15% require a photo ID. The pattern is similar for developed countries around the world."

The irony is that many liberal corporations decrying voter ID laws—as racist, as transphobic, and so on—require their employees to have ID. In fact, some of them have very strict ID requirements. In their own offices, IDs are no joke. They are absolutely required. As *Fox Business* has reported, "Over 200 US companies that called out changes to voter laws require ID for employment." Some companies even require customers to confirm their identity with a government-issued photo ID. Why? Because companies know that human beings break the rules. And they don't want just anyone entering the fold. Why is it any different when it comes to elections? Given their importance, shouldn't we be *more* stringent?

Unless of course, your candidates are benefitting from the absence of these laws.

As the novelist Upton Sinclair put it, "it is difficult to get a man to understand something when his salary depends upon his not understanding it."

If you're having trouble grasping why the DNC is so ardently against the kinds of commonsense, nonpartisan voter ID laws that every other country has when it comes to their elections, just come back to that quote.

If voter ID laws wiped out millions of conservative votes, every Democrat in Congress would be pushing hard for them. The *New York Times* and the *Washington Post* would be running story after story about election fraud. And the nonprofits, and the lawyers, they would be fighting tooth and nail to get voter ID on every state ballot. The Left might not be carrying the torch of morality, but they are carrying the torch of practicality. It's a practical advantage for them to keep our elections unsecure.

In reality, voting ID has nothing to do with racism, sexism, ableism, or any other kind of intolerance. It has everything to do with election integrity. It has everything to do with stopping the next steal. In that respect, it's not stripping anyone's voice. To the contrary, it's making sure that the voices of American citizens—rather than criminal illegal aliens—are heard.

Voter fraud is real.

That's why we have to beat the cheat by making each election too big to rig. Then, once we're in a position of power, we can change the laws and enact election integrity legislation.

At the end of 2025, three criminal illegal aliens were arrested for voting in Arkansas. As the attorney general's office explained: "Castellanos is a Cuban national who has a pending order of removal by an immigration judge from 1999. She also has three prior felony convictions in New York state. Her perjury charge stems from her marking on a voter registration form that she was a citizen of the United States and that she did not have any prior felony convictions. The election law violation arises from her illegally voting in the 2024 general election despite not being a U.S. citizen."

That same year, federal prosecutors brought charges against "a Colombian woman living illegally in Boston for 20 years under a stolen identity [who] voted in the 2024 election and improperly received more than $400,000 in federal benefits." In Taxachusetts, she "allegedly applied for a United States passport and obtained a Massachusetts Real ID and eight other state IDs." On November 5, 2024, she was caught on a bank surveillance camera wearing an "I voted" sticker.

In my neck of the woods, it was reported that "a New Jersey Democrat was hit with new charges regarding the alleged stealing and forging of ballots and voter registrations, and submissions of them in order to help him win a municipal election." And back in Minnesota, "a Minnesota election judge has been charged with allowing people who were not registered to vote to cast ballots in the 2024 election."

Around the same time, a woman in California was arraigned for registering her dog to vote in two different elections.

Yes, you read that correctly: her dog.

In one of those elections, the recall election of Governor Gavin Newsom, her dog's vote counted. The mail-in-ballot that counted was addressed to the dog. She posted a video of her dog on Facebook wearing an "I Voted" sticker.

In the America created by the Democrats, dogs are voting.

This might be funny if it was a *Saturday Night Live* sketch. It might even be funny if it was a vote for your favorite ice cream flavor at the local ice cream shop. I like a benign prank as much as the next person. It's not funny when it is our elections—and our democracy—that are at stake.

As FBI director Kash Patel has said, "voter fraud is a serious crime."

There's more than enough evidence to believe him.

In light of these examples, you would think every politician would want tougher voting laws. But the Democrats know that when criminal illegal aliens are allowed to vote, they stand a greater chance of winning the election. As John Nolte reported on October 15, 2025, "In March of 2023, Gov. Tim Walz (D-MN) signed a bill into law that allows illegal immigrants to receive a state driver's license. According to the far-left PolitiFact, about 81,000 people live in Minnesota illegally. And now we know why the unquestionably heterosexual Walz signed that law. . . . In a meeting of the Minnesota House this week, an election confirmed that this driver's license law allows illegal aliens to cast votes."

This is the sort of legislation that gets Republican politicians voted out of office.

This is the kind of lack of election integrity that prevents Republicans from winning office.

This is what will continue to make America Last.

If we want to win this country, we need to take a multiprong approach to elections. Voter registration is one prong. We need ballot harvesters. We need ballot chasers. We need people who are willing to put their boots on the ground and knock on doors. We need them all out there on the streets, on the farms, and in every other place where ballots can be secured. The Democrats had two thousand mules. I want two million mules.

But we also need election day workers. It's supposed to be one blue for every red; but imagine if reds just aren't inspired to become election day workers. And then you have seats that haven't been filled. So who fills them? The Democrats. The Democrats fill our seats because we didn't show up. It's a very real possibility that we could have election workers being 70 percent Democrat and 30 percent Republican because we didn't get enough people to leave their homes.

When we don't put in the work, when we don't care, it's legal for the Democrats to do that. It's legal for them to control our polling locations. We need eyes and ears inside of the polling locations to have safe and secure, fair and free elections. Right? Then why don't we make this a priority for every Republican organization in every state? These elections are too important for us to leave to the fickle winds of public trust.

If I had a dime for every time I heard one of my beautiful conservatives say it—"Scott, who counts the votes determines who wins the election"—I'd be a rich man. To these people, I ask: "Have you signed up to work at your polling location in Los Angeles?" "When was the last time you went online and typed in 'New York City election day worker' and put your name and number into the system so they'll call you and bring you on and have you as an election day worker?" "What polling location did you sign up to volunteer at in Boston?" "What shift are you working on November 4 in Philadelphia?"

After all, you just told me that who counts the votes determines who wins the election. I believe that. I love that. So let's get to work counting those votes!

If you're reading this book, my question is the same for you: Where are you signed up to be an election day volunteer in 2026?

(If you've made it this far through my book, I shouldn't even have to ask that other question: Are you registered to vote? If the answer is no, please put down this book immediately and visit EarlyVoteAction.com.)

We also need people monitoring to make sure that we're getting inactive voters removed and active voters that haven't voted for a long time to switch to inactive. It takes a multi-faceted, multi-layered, and multi-pronged approach in order to have election security and win an election. We need all of this. And we need it now.

As I have said before, this is the fight the Right needs to wage.

And this is the fight the Right needs to win—because, let's face it, the stakes have never been higher.

This is the fight that will determine the fate of the Republican Party in 2026, in 2028, and beyond.

Ultimately, it's the fight that will determine the future of the United States of America.

The 2028 Election

When I stepped foot inside the Oval Office after we won the election in 2024, I was blown away by President Trump's aura.

Here was a man who defied the political establishment—not just once, but twice.

Here was a man who had led the most successful presidential term in the history of the United States of America, the greatest country on planet earth.

Here was a man who was back in office, just the second president in US history to win a nonsequential election, and he was already making America greater than it has ever been.

It was February 27, 2025, when I made my way to Capitol Hill, and President Trump was already securing our border, making the world economy once again work for Americans, and otherwise draining the swamp in our nation's capital.

When I stood with the president, I truly felt his aura: that indomitable American spirit, that ambience that has gripped millions of Americans that, frankly, can't be fully described in words.

But there was another man whose presence I felt in the Oval Office, a man who has been with President Trump since day one.

He is a man of absolute credibility, and absolute loyalty, who is right by President Trump's side Making America Great Again.

His name is JD Vance.

I can say that he is not only the best vice president in American history, he is the future of the MAGA movement when President Trump leaves office in 2028.

I mean, seriously, is there anyone else who understands the stakes of our movement better than Vice President Vance? Is there anyone else who understands what needs to be done in our country and around the world? Is there anyone else who can lead us in 2028 and beyond?

I love the politicians in the MAGA movement, and I have proudly worked with many of them. Believe me when I say it, we have the most talented and virtuous political movement in American history. And I'm grateful we have so many beautiful leaders committed to our cause.

But Vice President JD Vance is really in a league of his own.

He's President Trump's righthand man, he knows what needs to be done on the border, he knows how we address the failures of national intelligence, he knows how to bring manufacturing back to this country, including the great state of Ohio where he is from, and as a veteran of the US Marines he knows what we need to do to make the US military great again.

Could we have asked for a better leader in 2028?

As JD Vance told the world on July 17, 2024, at the Republican National Convention in the great state of Wisconsin: "Tonight is a night of hope. A celebration of what America once was, and with God's grace, what it will soon be again. And it is a reminder of the sacred duty we have to preserve the American experiment, to choose a new path for our children and grandchildren. . . . My message to you, my fellow Republicans, is—we love this country and we are united to win."

In 2028, I will be fighting for JD Vance.

I will be fighting for the America First movement.

And after the greatest president the United States has ever seen leaves office, I will be fighting to Keep America Great.

Will you join me in this fight?

If you've learned anything from this book, I want you to know that with hard work, a dream—and, dare I say it, *persistence*—you can go from the doghouse to the White House.

Game on.

ACKNOWLEDGMENTS

I wouldn't be here—quite literally—if it wasn't for my parents. They taught me to work hard, to serve others, and to never stop fighting for what is right and true in the world, even when the odds are stacked against you. Without my father and mother, Captain Robert Presler and Carol Presler, I would not be The Persistence.

To my team at Early Vote Action, you all are amazing. Each and every day, I am impressed by the work that you do. I am impressed by your resolute focus to Make America Great Again. We won Pennsylvania, and I know that—with your courage, intelligence, and commitment to the movement—we are going to continue to win.

Without President Donald J. Trump, America would not be on its path back to greatness. From the bottom of my heart, there is no one who deserves my gratitude more than this political outsider who inspired a new movement to reshape the United States and the world. Mr. President, we are with you until the end!

Finally, Jesus Christ said, "With man this is impossible, but with God all things are possible." I am forever grateful to God for the life I live, and the strength he gives me to fight day in and day out for the future of our Christian nation.